English#Heritage

Book of

Tintagel

Arthur and Archaeology

..237

English # Heritage
Book of
Tintagel
Arthur and Archaeology

Charles Thomas

B.T. Batsford Ltd / English Heritage
London

First published 1993

Typeset by Goodfellow & Egan, Cambridge
and printed in Great Britain by
The Bath Press, Bath

Published by B T Batsford Ltd
4 Fitzhardinge Street, London W1H 0AH

A CIP catalogue record for this book is available
from the British Library

ISBN 0 7134 6689 8 (cased)
ISBN 0 7134 6690 1 (limp)

Contents

Illustrations

Colour plates

Acknowledgements

Any account of Tintagel, a complex of archaeological sites where active research continues, can only be an interim statement – a personal one, drawing on the findings and ideas of many people. My greatest debt is to colleagues whose interest and involvement have provided so many ideas – Professors Leslie Alcock, Rosemary Cramp, Peter Fowler, Michael Fulford, Christopher Morris, Philip Rahtz and Malcolm Todd – and equally to those, mainly from Cornwall Archaeological Unit, who in the last few years did the actual work in the field – Nic Appleton-Fox, Colleen Batey, Chris Crowe and Stephen Hartgroves. Very special thanks must be reserved for Jacqueline Nowakowski, director of the Churchyard excavations in 1990–1, and Carl Thorpe, who has also acted as my research assistant and draughtsman. There is not room to name everybody else in the archaeological world who has helped, but I ask them to accept the same warm thanks. Our general debt to the public relations division of Mobil North Sea Limited (especially to Christopher Patey, Keith King and Lloyd Slater) is apparent in the fact that such completely unexpected progress in excavation and publication could be made at all. For the provision since 1985 of expert new surveys, site plans and a full photographic record we all thank most warmly the staff – friends and colleagues – of the Royal Commission on the Historical Monuments of England (in which I have served as a Commissioner since 1983) and its successive Secretaries, Peter Fowler and Tom Hassall.

All our work at Tintagel was made doubly pleasurable and successful through the continued kindness and assistance of so many good friends there – the Vicar, Reverend Ivan Gregory, Derek Flew and his staff, the Parochial Church Council, the communities at Tintagel and Treknow, and notably English Heritage's custodial, industrial and maintenance staff at Tintagel and elsewhere in Cornwall. Their interest, care for the visible past and endless practical help on site have been major contributions to all recent research. I am myself also grateful to others in Tintagel – Mike Goff (Minerals and Fossils Museum), Mike Godwin, Don Hutchinson and Peter Saville (King Arthur's Great Halls of Chivalry) and Fred Whiting OBE (both County Councillor and churchwarden) – for friendly and unstinted help.

For the illustrations: I particularly thank my daughter Susanna for specialist photographs, Carl Thorpe for the use of numerous drawings of finds, and Tracey Croft (English Heritage) for her plans and the chapel reconstruction (**88**).

Finally, it is only proper to point out two things that colour the whole text. My affection and respect for Dr C.A. Ralegh Radford, who figures prominently here, remain undiminished throughout forty years. It gives me no pleasure to disagree with his ideas and conclusions; I do so because the results of later work have made it impossible for me to accept them, and I hope that Chapters 4 and 6 in particular show how much is owed to his pioneer research. Secondly, in a personal account I have included a good many personal views and opinions. My prolonged involvement with Tintagel, privately and officially, and a concern for the monument's future that we must all share, allow me to write these. They must not however be taken to reflect the official views of either the Duchy of Cornwall or English Heritage.

Cornwall, August 1992

1

Space, time and discourses

The founder and editor of the journal *Antiquity*, the late O.G.S. Crawford, used to tell the tale of a Victorian antiquary who dug up a Roman villa and published his findings. In his excitement, he quite forgot to say where the villa was . . . The present author, who for all his life has been excited about Tintagel, often has to remind himself that a lot of people do not know how to pronounce this place-name correctly – Tin-*tadj*-el, with an emphasis on the middle bit, as in 'imagine' – or could pin-point it on a map. We begin then with a collection of plain facts to save readers the bother of having to look them up elsewhere. Those who are still interested can then read on, when they will be told much else: the story of Tintagel, up to Midsummer 1992.

Nowadays, each year about a quarter of a million people visit Tintagel by design or by accident. Most are British, most are on holiday. A very much greater number of folk have heard of King Arthur, if only in connection with the Round Table, the Knights and the sword called Excalibur. A survey in August 1988 revealed that nearly half the visitors had come because of the Arthurian link (not the archaeology), and some will have been able to get a drink in a hotel whose side-door has EXCALIBAR above it. In reality, Arthur's connection with Tintagel is historically less meaningful than Sir Winston Churchill's with Fulton, Missouri. However, it is there; it will not go away; and this book is not being written for specialists in medieval literature nor for that matter primarily for historians and archaeologists. It is for all those who have been to Tintagel, but were unable to find answers to many obvious questions, and equally for those who have not yet made the visit.

Space

Tintagel is the name of an ecclesiastical parish, and now also of the principal village within it, at map reference (NGR) SX 050 890 on the north coast of Cornwall (**1**). The parish is a large one, of 1735 ha (4281 acres). It has 5 km (3 miles) of rugged coastline and several thousand inhabitants. Until the 1920s its economy was based upon agriculture and the quarrying of roofing-slates; it rests now on tourism, a short annual season during which takings must be maximized, and a decreasing element of farming. The village's real name is Trevena or Trevenna (this is from the Cornish language: *tre war veneth* 'the farm-holding on the hillside') but in 1900, when the telegraph arrived and the postal system was updated, its name was quietly replaced in what one of the National Trust guidebooks has described as 'a flash of marketing genius worthy of twentieth-century promotional methods'. What was being marketed was a blend of coastal scenery and sea air replete with ozone, believed to be good for tired city lungs, and also the idea of King Arthur made famous through the poems of Alfred Lord Tennyson.

Tintagel is not on the way to anywhere, though you pass it by following a minor coastal road. It is reached by a network of such minor roads, all now well-maintained but until the 1930s notoriously rough, that run north-west off the A39, the principal trunk road down the northern side of Cornwall. In the 1890s William Taylor JP, a true son of Tintagel whose own guidebook will be cited later, built an enormous hotel on Fire Beacon Cliff, the most prominent headland just beyond Trevena village. It can be seen for miles, and at a distance is frequently mistaken for Tintagel Castle (**2**). Its resem-

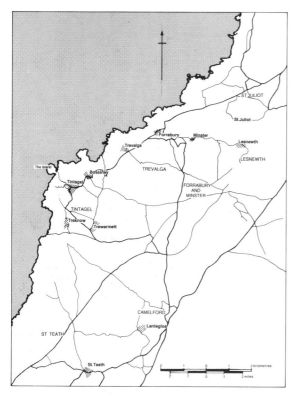

1 *Location map of the Tintagel district.*

2 *King Arthur's Castle Hotel; architect, Sylvanus Trevail, 1895–9* (photo: author).

blance to a railway hotel like Gleneagles or Tregenna Castle is no accident. Mr Taylor, who had irons in many fires, was scheming to get a rail loop, a tourist branch-line, run out from the former London and South Western Railway between Camelford and Delabole. This failed, as did another attempt in the 1920s. William Taylor had meanwhile built an anticipatory golf course, modifying but not destroying a handsome set of terraced medieval fields, those of the original Trevena farm. They can be viewed now from the turning-bay just before the hotel entrance. The railway line has long since gone, and so has the former most-of-Cornwall bus network. Without cars Tintagel would once again be isolated.

What visitors go to see is Tintagel Castle, a jumble of slate-walled ruins of the thirteenth century, partly on the isolated headland called Tintagel *Island*, and partly on the adjoining mainland cliffside (3). Many also visit the parish church, dedicated to God in the name of St Materiana (or Matheriana, or Mertheriana). An area around the Castle, with the whole of the Island, forms part of the Crown estate of the Duchy of Cornwall. This is by no means the same as the modern administrative *county* of Cornwall; the Duchy owns almost all of the Isles of Scilly, much of Dartmoor, isolated parts of Cornwall and individual estates in Wiltshire, Somerset, inner London and elsewhere. The title of this dukedom adheres automatically to the eldest son of a reigning monarch at his birth, or else when a parent succeeds as king or queen. This has meant that the title is not necessarily continuous. Its present and twenty-ninth holder, H.R.H. Charles Philip Arthur George, Prince of Wales, became Duke of Cornwall at birth on 14 November, 1948. When he is in Cornwall or Scilly, Prince Charles prefers to be known as 'The Duke of Cornwall' (which pleases the Cornish). The first such Duke was Edward the Black Prince, son of King Edward III, created on 16 March, 1337. Before that date there was a Norman earldom of Cornwall. It had nothing whatsoever to do with a fictional, or imaginary, series of earls from pre-Norman

3 *(Top) Dr William Borlase's view of Tintagel Island and Castle from the east (in his* Observations on the Antiquities . . . of . . . Cornwall, *Oxford 1754). (*Below*) the same view in 1989 (photo: RCHME).*

4 *Tintagel parish church (St Materiana), from the south-east side (*photo: RCHME*).*

days. The first Earl was either the Breton count Alan (before 1140) or possibly his uncle, Brian of Brittany.

The manor of Tintagel, originally the manor of Bossiney – the name of a hamlet just east of Tintagel village – was acquired in 1233–6 by Richard, third (or fourth) Earl of Cornwall, son of King John. Seven hundred and sixty years on, the Duchy still holds Tintagel Castle, legal possessor of the site and of anything found within it or adhering to the soil. The care and upkeep of an ancient place where nobody lives, which has no practical use, and which countless numbers of people want to visit, is costly and burdensome. Since 1929 the care of the Castle has been transferred by the Duchy to those agencies of government set up to deal with such problems; through this route it is now in the charge of English Heritage who have the responsibility for its care and upkeep. They aim to provide safe and convenient access, custodial staff, a shop, ticket office and full interpretative facilities for young and old.

The other principal monument at Tintagel is the parish church (Church of England) (4). Smaller and slightly older than the remains of the Castle, this church in regard to its worship is and long has been doctrinally High. Within the parish are worshippers of the other denominations – mostly Wesleyan Methodist and Roman Catholic – but the church of St Materiana also serves as a symbol of the whole parish as a community, and of the corporate identity of Tintagel.

There is by now a vast literature about every aspect of Tintagel, from its geology through Arthuriana to sea-birds and ferns, much of it in the shape of guidebooks or what a librarian might class as Topographical Visits. The place is lucky to have a detailed history of outstanding worth, *The Parish of Tintagel* by the Reverend Arthur C. Canner, vicar from 1950 to 1977. Canner's book (1982) has now been re-issued (1992), and its existence makes it unnecessary to repeat here a mass of fully-documented information from primary and secondary sources.

If you were lucky enough to fly over Tintagel in a small plane, easily the best way to appreciate the relationship of the high coastline, the broad coastal farming belt, and the ground rising inland to Bodmin Moor, you would at once ask: Where, apart from the Castle, are all the archaeological remains? The landscape is parcelled out into fields large and small, some of which may have been enclosed a thousand years ago. The archaeology is nearly all coastal. Excavations organized by the Office of Works took place at the Castle and Island, on and off, in the period 1933–8. There was more work on a reduced scale in 1942 (churchyard) and in 1956 (the Castle's Great Ditch), and again throughout the 1980s under the aegis of successive government agencies. In 1990 and 1991 limited excavation on the Island (Site C – see **43**) was directed for English Heritage by Professor Christopher Morris of the University of Glasgow. At the same time, there were excavations within Tintagel parish churchyard. These were undertaken by a team representing the Cornwall Archaeological Unit (CAU) from Truro, and the Institute of Cornish Studies (University of Exeter and Cornwall County Council). They were sponsored by Mobil North Sea Limited. Resumption in 1993 or later will depend on available funds and further sponsorship. Neither excavation was on an extended scale. Both produced remarkable results. With the opportunity to describe other and related aspects of Tintagel (church, parish, sites and the district) as something of inherent interest to ordinary folk, those results provide sufficient reason for a new book.

Time – an archaeological time-scale by periods

This is the reader's guide to the last two thousand years at Tintagel. It can reflect only what historians and archaeologists think probably took place and is therefore, like all such passages, in the nature of an interim report. In what follows 'the Island' means Tintagel Island with the adjoining cove or Haven and also that small part of the adjacent mainland containing the landward wards of the Castle. 'Churchyard' is Tintagel parish churchyard, with the church, and also a small area around it of unknown extent. 'The district' is a part-circle, with the Island as centre and a radius of about 8 km or 5 miles, extending inland.

Prehistory – Period 0

Nothing prehistoric can be assigned to either the Island or the churchyard. The prehistory of the whole district is most imperfectly known anyhow, and because Cornwall's centre-of-population, main towns, active archaeological societies and active fieldworkers all lie much further westward, this district has not been fully investigated. A few small chips of flint, some worked, have over the years been picked up from pathways on the Island. They cannot possibly be held to show any real prehistoric

occupation. There are cliff castles, or promontory forts, along the coast, such as a prominent one at Willapark near Boscastle (SX 062 898), and conceivably some slight remains at Barras Nose (SX 053 894). Though unexcavated these can be assigned to the pre-Roman Iron Age (the last five centuries BC, the early first century AD) because similar forts in Cornwall have been excavated and thus dated. One interesting facet of Tintagel's Island (and neck) as a once narrow promontory is that it was apparently *not* used to make any sort of prehistoric cliff defensive work.

Roman period – Period I

Historical evidence comes in the shape of two inscribed Late Roman (third- and fourth-century) milestones or route-markers, one found at the churchyard entrance (**5**) and the other (**6**) from beyond Bossiney (p. 82), indicating a north coast route of some kind that may have terminated at the Camel estuary opposite Padstow. The archaeological evidence comes so far only from the Island and is in the form of small finds. There are sherds of fourth-century Roman wheelmade pottery, notably of a type known as Oxford Red Colour-coated ware. There are also a good many sherds of locally made jars and bowls, which from their shape, fabric and rare ornamentation would be assigned to the Late Roman period too; unless, of course, these were still circulating a century afterwards. A small parcel of Roman coins, apparently found in a shrivelled purse within the landward wards (p. 84), is also relevant.

As for the churchyard – where post-Roman activity and the first signs of Christianity date from around AD 500 (or soon after that), there is at the very least a suspicion that there may also have been a pre-Christian burial area involving stone-lined graves and, if so, probably falling within Period I (p. 102).

Post-Roman – Period II

The post-Roman Period II starts in the fifth century AD. There is no agreed name for this phase of Britain's past. Choice of label depends on where you are: 'Pagan Saxon', for instance, would be appropriate in East Anglia but at this date ridiculous in remote Cornwall. Much previous literature has presented Tintagel's Period II as 'Dark Age' or even as 'Arthurian'. It is, comparatively, the very reverse of Dark, since a huge quantity of finds and even structures is

13

5 *Roman milestone (found incorporated in the lychgate, 1889) at Tintagel church. It reads: IMPCG VAL LIC LICIN ('The emperor Caesar, Galerius Valerius Licinianus Licinius', emperor AD 308–24) (photo: Susanna Thomas).*

6 *Roman milestone at Trethevy, Tintagel. It reads: IMP C DOMI NGAL LOET VOLVS ('The Emperors Gallus and Volusianus', emperors AD 251–3) (photo: Susanna Thomas).*

under constant interpretation, and 'Arthurian' begs the question of whether a historical as opposed to a literary Arthur ever existed, where in Britain his career should be located and precisely when he lived. 'Post-Roman' is put forward because the inferred material culture, events and even the anonymous personalities of Period II at Tintagel are more readily linked to the preceding Late Roman empire, in Britain and elsewhere, than to the English conquests in southern and eastern Britain.

On the Island, Period II covers a major but not necessarily unbroken occupation attested by finds, domestic constructions and a defensive work. Up to what date this continued remains a matter for cautious estimate. At the moment (1992) our interpretation of this archaeology rules out occupation much after AD 600; there is no obviously seventh-century material. At the churchyard, where Period II does continue and merges into Period III, there is

the associated sacred place, linked by finds to the occupation of the Island, used for Christian burial and perhaps also worship (p. 103).

Historically, there *are* Period II sources of a kind, but they concern much larger regions of early Britain. An example – the nature of the Period II use of the Island, with its evidence of temporal wealth and power, would suggest that it was controlled by figures who could be described as kings, not of what became Cornwall, but of a wider south-west British kingdom known as *Dumnonia*. Mainly from Wales there are later Lives of early British saints, fragmentary annals or chronicles purporting to cover the distant past, and even collections of genealogies or of regnal lists, successions of named rulers. Some provide the names of Dumnonian kings who, if they really lived and reigned, belong to Period II. But none of these sources mentions Tintagel, or any place identifiable as Tintagel, or anywhere within Cornwall representing a royal capital in the medieval sense.

Late Pre-Conquest (and Early Norman) – Period III

This is an unusual, and by now unusually interesting, division of time past, a definition of which seems to be necessary at Tintagel though possibly not elsewhere. Period III ends about AD 1230, when Earl Richard's castle was built. However, on the Island, if the end of Period II is taken as around 600, there may have been quite a long stage of virtual desertion. At least one feature, the little Chapel, is certainly older than 1230 and aspects of it may go back to the eleventh century. The churchyard, judging from the 1990–1 excavations, exhibits a great deal of (pre-1230) Period III use. There is the parish church itself, commenced in the early twelfth century; traces of a smaller and older church alongside it of about AD 1000, its foundations incorporating pieces of a still earlier church (of about 950?); and various graves that must be assigned to stages in the period between the seventh and thirteenth centuries. In the district there are stone crosses, plain and inscribed, of Period III. As for secular sites, there are traces of Norman ringworks or mottes, all not much later than the Conquest, at Boscastle, Bossiney and Castle Goff near Lanteglos.

There is a historical setting for Period III. The phase must include the domination, tenurial changes and considerable expansion of agricultural settlement introduced into this part of Cornwall by Christian English. The Domesday Book survey of 1086 is a prime source because it names pre-1066 landowners. And finally, though not historical in quite the same sense, the first allusions to Tintagel as a stronghold of Cornish kings and noblemen fall within Period III. The saga of King Mark, Tristan and Iseult harks back to a purely legendary past, rooted in Period II. Geoffrey of Monmouth's writings (in the 1130s) introduced Arthur to Tintagel, and therefore are the unwitting foundations of subsequent associations.

The Castle – Period IV

This period is relevant to the Island alone. It embraces the short existence of the Castle as any kind of functional strongpoint. It begins with its construction, falling within 1230–40 (p. 118), and ends with the early sixteenth century, by which time the Castle had long ceased to have any military meaning. The archaeology, or the structural sequence of alterations and additions, of the Castle remains to be worked out, because so much of the monument is missing, and the corresponding history – patchy as it is – must be gleaned from occasional mentions in the accounts of the Earldom and (after 1337) the Duchy.

Post-medieval to the present – Period V

This final stage – everything from about 1530 to now – might be labelled post-medieval and recent. It concerns us mostly for its human and literary interest. The Castle was perceived and depicted as a spectacular ruin, crying out for the pen of any poet and the pencil of any artist, with Arthurian associations. Tintagel church, and churchyard, has its own separate and unbroken history throughout Periods IV and V, adequately documented. It would be permissible to claim that Period V came to a somewhat exhausted finale in the decade 1970–80 because since then, through analysis of known finds and renewed digging, the appreciation of Tintagel's archaeological past makes it impossible to go back to what, during Period V, were the accepted ideas about Tintagel's history.

Discourses

Almost every visible part of Tintagel could be said to offer 'a discourse'. The word possesses, here, much more than its normal dictionary meaning. A discourse (and this is now rather an in-word among theoretical archaeologists) comprises some intended public statement or utterance, but not a spoken one, aimed at a receptive target or audience who are expected to be able to decipher its content. Wander around any large municipal cemetery of the nineteenth century; look at the ornate tombstones of city fathers, captains of industry or similar once-important people. Their size, the use of expensive imported marble, the many lines of writing, addition of honours after a name, and such accessories as black iron chains, urns, granite chippings and stout kerbs, all make up a discourse. The message underlines the importance and the significance of the dead man, and also of his surviving relations. 'Look at the money we can afford to spend' and 'Our kind of people deserve this kind of memorial' is the content. We, as the less fortunate strollers through God's acre, are the audience and target. The dead do not speak. In this case, they do not need to speak to us because their

discourse is conveyed in another fashion.

What makes a study of Tintagel as a set of great monuments in part artificial, in part natural, so fascinating is the gradual discovery of layer upon layer of hidden discourses. Now it would be perfectly possible to write a dry-as-dust account of Tintagel and its archaeology, describing all the sites and all the finds and putting all the events in an A to Z order, and then offering a series of rather timid interpretations – in case future discoveries upset today's theories – but to do so would be to miss the point altogether. There were discourses in the remote past, just as meaningful as today's.

At Tintagel, the physical setting makes up a large part of the discourse in each case. There has been a renewed interest recently in Britain's castles, elaborate fortresses of stone and masonry from Norman to Elizabethan times and, along with cathedrals and major churches, the largest surviving monuments that we can inspect. When historians and historical geographers join the discussion, we begin to learn more about the siting of castles in the landscape, strategy instead of small-scale tactics, the impressive economy of castle-building, and the part played by fortification in political and dynastic power games.

There are castles of this kind in Cornwall (7). There is the very early, and strategically vital, castle at Launceston commanding a river Tamar crossing, the so-called Gateway to Cornwall; or Restormel, a shell-keep by Lostwithiel at the first place where an east–west highway can cross the river Fowey; and the rather later castles of Pendennis and St Mawes, designed to guard both sides of the long natural harbour flanked by modern Falmouth. It does not need a military historian nor a strategist to suggest that, alongside these, Tintagel Castle had no military value or function whatsoever. A hundred enemy ships, keeping a cable's length offshore, could sail by with impunity. Armies could march past, inland, without being challenged. No commander in his right mind would dream of landing a force at Tintagel Haven.

7 *Eastern Cornwall (from the map in the Lysons brothers'* Magna Britannia, *vol. iii, 1814) with the four great Earldom, later Duchy, castles –* Launceston (*top right*), *Trematon* (*bottom right*), *Restormel* (*bottom left*) *and away from all the strategic routes,* Tintagel (*on the coast, top left*).

None of the three ancient routes down the spine of Cornwall runs anywhere near Tintagel.

If this castle cannot be explained in military terms, it is necessary to dig a little deeper. The discourse offered by the very existence of Earl Richard's coastal citadel is itself layered, and seven and a half centuries later is not very easy to read, but it can still be guessed. Richard, born in 1209 as the second son of King John, lived in the public gaze. It can have been no secret that in 1233, when he was only 24 – and he would, later, be regarded as one of the richest men in the kingdom – he was intending to give three of the Earldom of Cornwall's manors (good land, too; one near the Devon border and two further west) to Gervase de Hornicote in exchange for the solitary coastal manor of Bossiney, which included Tintagel Island. Richard's brother King Henry III confirmed this exchange in 1236. It is possible to make out, approximately, what took place. Richard had persuaded Gervase to hand over Bossiney and Tintagel to him. Gervase, whose own family had held Bossiney for three or four generations after the Conquest, styled himself (or was known locally as) Gervase *de Tyntagel*. This does not mean that he lived there – the family home, now Hornacott in North Tamerton, is nearly 32 km (20 miles) away – but it does suggest the growing fame of Tintagel as a place, and not that of an otherwise undistinguished family. A curious aspect of the initial sale in May of 1233 is that it mentions Gervase's 'island of Tyntagel' *and* 'the Castle of Richard', as if under some informal and unrecorded previous agreement the building may already have started. Earl Richard may in fact have put his idea into effect in 1230, when he became 21.

Richard – vain, ambitious, physically weak – had been created Earl of Cornwall in May 1227. He was literate and educated, and unusually spoke and read English as well as Norman-French and Latin. How many times he visited Tintagel before and after acquiring the manor is not known; but probably very few. But this, with its Island, was the place named in Geoffrey of Monmouth's *History of the Kings of Britain* as the seat of earls and dukes of Cornwall, long before the Normans arrived. Gorlois, whose wife Igerna was Arthur's mother, was a *dux*, Duke, here. And in other stories, not all of which may have survived complete, still

8 *Tintagel Castle – a view from Island to the mainland with* (foreground) *reconstructed 'Site F' and the wall of the Inner Ward and, across the neck at the top of the steps, the Lower Ward on the left and the crag-like Upper Ward to the right* (photo: RCHME).

greater men had ruled from Tintagel; men like King Mark, the uncle of Prince Tristan, to whom Cornwall if not also Brittany had been subject. Conquerors seek to embellish their power by acquiring the principal seats of conquered leaders – in the 1940s it was rumoured that Adolf Hitler had his eye on Windsor Castle, Balmoral, even Buckingham Palace. The comparison is not really fair to Richard, who was legitimately created Cornwall's earl, but the motive was similar. By 1236, the pointless yet conspicuous Castle of Tintagel (**8**) must have been well-nigh completed, involving great cost and a large resident workforce. Its presence constituted a statement in stone, a message, a discourse, and the intended audience was of course the (largely indifferent?) Cornish people and perhaps Richard's critics elsewhere. If it can still be read, the message was: 'Gaze on the stronghold of the earl of Cornwall, *your* earl

– Here of old you yourselves claim that *your* kings and earls held sway before the Normans came – Where else, save at Tintagel, would you expect me to reconstruct my seat?' And even today the visitor who realizes that the strategic aspect of the place is immaterial, because Tintagel Castle is more fittingly described as a folly, will be able to share just a little in Richard's intended discourse.

The parish church

A final instance of a discourse is provided by Tintagel parish church. Perhaps its most striking characteristic is the siting (**9**). It stands on a slight rise of the cliff-land, Glebe Cliff as it is known, a good half-mile from the village of Trevena or Tintagel. There is no indication that it stood in some now-vanished settlement and the immediate question is *why* does it stand where it does, instead of being in the centre of the village like most Cornish church-town villages? The historian would point out that, from architectural evidence, the church was probably built about 1120–40, and is therefore earlier than the village, where the main street (Fore Street) represents plots and dwellings lining the track down to the valley, with its mill,

9 *Tintagel parish church, seen from the village's main street half a mile away (*photo: author*).*

alongside the Castle dating to 1230–6.

The church is dedicated in the name of a St Materiana, whom the medieval Cornish took to have been female; there are other spellings of her name but 'Materiana' will do for the moment. The church appears to have been planned (**10**) as a cruciform, a ground-plan like a blunt cross – chancel, longer nave, north and south transepts – and the first design may have been to have a central tower over the crossing. If so, this was abandoned and the present west tower is an addition, stylistically dated to the fourteenth century. The first church, as it stood completed about 1140, was a handsome one and like some other Norman churches in Cornwall the most spectacular doorway would have been at the west end. On the assumption that it was probably a round-headed doorway with several orders of chevron or dogtooth ornament, a careful look-out was kept during the 1990–1 churchyard excavations. All loose pieces of worked greenstone were examined and, sure enough, several tell-tale fragments of such ornamentation (flung aside when the fourteenth-century tower was added) were found in disturbed contexts (**11**).

The centre of the cult of St Materiana, the older church that claimed to have this saint's tomb, was a few miles north-eastward at Minster, the mother-church of Boscastle. The size and scale of Tintagel church as a new building of the early twelfth century point to founders of wealth and importance, and founders connected with Boscastle. If so, these must have been the Norman lords of the place, the family of De Boterel or Bottreaux, who are first recorded there about 1130 and who may well have been granted Boscastle by 1100. Their name is perpetuated in that of the village, with its narrow natural harbour and long main street snaking up the valley – Boscastle was *Boterelescastel* in 1302. The castle did exist. It has long gone, but the massive motte or semi-artificial mound on which it stood can still be detected, on the north-east side of the valley. When the Bottreaux family took over this fief, they also took over the lay proprietorship of the ancient church of Minster (p. 109).

Tintagel church is approximately in the centre of a coastal belt scattered with any number of hamlets, joined up by roads and now also, regrettably, by unsympathetic modern development. The names of most hamlets, beginning with Cornish *tre(v)* – ('farm-holding')

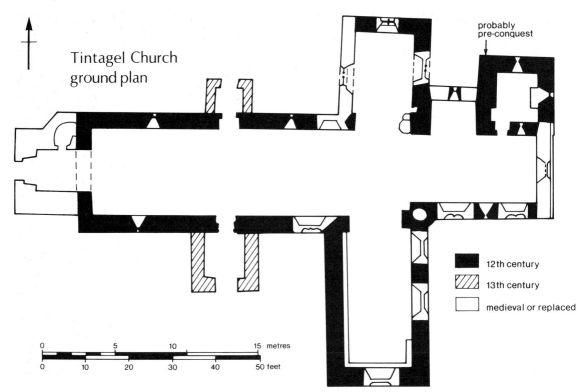

probably
pre-conquest

Tintagel Church
ground plan

0   5   10   15 metres
0 10 20 30 40 50 feet

■ 12th century

▨ 13th century

□ medieval or replaced

10 *Tintagel parish church – ground plan (*after Edmund H. Sedding*).*

– are as old as Norman times (at least); Trevena itself, Trebissoms, Trecarn, Treven, Trevillick, Trenale, etc; there are plenty more of them. In the twelfth century they housed a population in the hundreds. As will be shown, this population did not lack the equivalent of a parish church (p. 108), but it was a fairly insignificant one. We do not possess, eight centuries later, the documentary sources that might guide us; but we can guess that for some reason or other the Bottreaux family intended to furnish the area with a large and impressive new church, endowed with a relic of St Materiana from Minster.

Where, here, is any discourse? The answer has to be: in the nature of the church itself. Only part of the outward message would be concerned with the greater glory of God, because the rest of it is a type of social advertisement – to the piety, the generosity and the wealth of the Lord of Boterelescastel, a man who (at home) controlled the older church and shrine of the important St Materiana and a man in a position to erect as handsome a

church as the next baron. This reading can be supported by drawing attention to an odd little room, or cell, or chapel – sometimes called 'the Lady Chapel' – squeezed into the north-east angle of the ground-plan cross. This has been explained as an addition in the thirteenth century. To find the solution it would all have to be taken to pieces, but there is a distinct possibility that one of its walls (preferably the thick, battered, *west* wall) was there already as the *east* wall of a smaller and older building; that the little round-headed slit windows were reused; and that it was really a pre-1120 secondary church or chapel of some kind deliberately incorporated in the Norman cruciform. If so, its function must have been as a chantry. This was a special part of the church, where an endowed priest – not necessarily the vicar – could daily say Masses for the repose of the souls of William de Bottreaux and his family. Minster church, which is smaller, shows no signs of any such endowed chantry aspect.

These details, with fuller descriptions and the archaeological background, will be returned to in Chapters 6 and 7. They are mentioned here to demonstrate, not the importance of archaeology as a mode of unlocking the past,

20

11 *(Left) Tintagel churchyard, 1991; an expected fragment of the ornate Norman west doorway, destroyed when the later tower was added (photo: author). (Above) South doorway of Kilkhampton church, Cornwall, to show what the doorway might have looked like (photo: RCHME).*

but the complexity of a process that is increasingly seen as necessary if we are ever to understand the past as a product of human nature. And that means human nature with all such pardonable attributes as self-esteem, vanity, piety and ostentation. In London, the Albert Memorial on the southern edge of Hyde Park is a pretty fair instance of this. When we look deeply, we can easily learn to interpret past doings that have left their mark, and forgotten constructions, as 'discourses' between those who caused them to appear, and those who saw or touched or visited or used them.

12 *Tintagel parish church. The twelfth-century north doorway showing the plain tympanum (above the door) and dragonesque iron hinges (*sketch by Edmund H. Sedding, 1902*).*

Obviously, as a visit today will show, there are almost certainly other and older factors detectable at Tintagel church and churchyard. Attributing its building to the Bottreaux family does not answer all the questions. Today it is the *south* doorway with its added medieval porch that forms the main entrance, and it is approached by the lane from the village, past the medieval vicarage, which ends by a *south* entrance and stile through the churchyard wall. In the twelfth century, apart from a splendiferous double- or triple-ordered round-headed west doorway, the nave of the Norman church had a *north* door (**12**). This was certainly more important than any contemporary south-side entrance; it has a semicircular (blank) tympanum above it, chamfered jambs, and probably a stout oaken door with ornate dragonesque wrought-iron hinges. The door perished centuries ago. The hinges, unless they are perhaps thirteenth–fourteenth-century replacement copies of the originals, are still there. A north doorway would open out in the direction of the Castle. In 1140, the Castle did not exist, and would not be built until 1230 or so. Another reason has to be found for this north-side emphasis (p. 105).

These are not merely ecclesiological ramblings. Like much else about the past at Tintagel, they confront us with minor mysteries. The purpose of the present book is not, alas, to offer final answers to all such mysteries. Neither is it to bore the reader with page after page of detailed archaeology when he or she wants the conclusions instead of the nuts-and-bolts. The writer's wish is to share with others the excitement of a campaign of discovery that started in earnest a long time ago, and is still unfinished.

2

Magical conceptions, modern misconceptions

The legacy of Geoffrey of Monmouth

It is pleasant to sit on the Island during a summer's afternoon and to imagine what stories could have been told about Tintagel before the twelfth century. Nothing in writing has survived to guide us. What *is* probable, however, is that the connection with King Arthur begins – as far as we know – with the appearance in 1135–8 of a *History of the Kings of Britain, 'Historia Regum Britanniae'*, written by Geoffrey of Monmouth. Geoffrey is described as a Normanized Celt, perhaps of Breton descent, and that sums up most of what is known of him. He began his *History* some time before 1135 and there is a strong likelihood that he had visited Cornwall and had seen Tintagel for himself. The *History* attempted to provide an account of Britain, from pre-Roman times up to the age when the native British had been conquered by the Saxons, the English, and the whole character of the land and its nation had been changed. Geoffrey was obsessed with a legendary Arthur, once ruler of Britain, and much of his book has an Arthurian emphasis.

The place-name *Tintagol* does not appear before the twelfth century. It is an *oppidum*, a fortress, somewhere in the province of Cornwall standing *in litore maris* 'on the sea-shore', and we encounter Gorlois, duke of Cornwall as its possessor. This takes place in post-Roman days, Period II of the previous chapter, when the king of all Britain was Uther Pendragon. King Uther summons all his provincial dukes and lords to celebrate Easter with him at London and there the beautiful wife of Gorlois, Igerna, attracts her monarch's notice; to an unwelcome degree, since Gorlois departs in anger taking his wife back to Cornwall with him. When Uther's summons to return has

been received and ignored, Gorlois has to face an invasion of Cornwall by the lovesick king with his army. Duke Gorlois therefore places Igerna at Tintagel, his most secure refuge and stronghold, and himself retires to another fortress called *Dimilioc*. Insofar as any of this is real, Dimilioc represents a smaller hillfort inland, 32 km (20 miles) south of Tintagel, now occupied (at grid reference SW 951 583) by the parish church of St Dennis – it was within an estate listed as *Dimelihoc* in Domesday Book.

At this stage in Geoffrey's narrative a point is reached from which, for centuries, Arthurian perceptions (or misconceptions) about Tintagel have flowed. Uther besieges Dimilioc; he cannot capture it and a week later he confesses to his friend Ulfin that he is sick with love for Igerna. What should he do? Ulfin explains to the king that there would be no point in abandoning the siege and marching on Tintagel – where, we suppose, Igerna's presence had become known – because it was impossible to break into the castle of Tintagel. 'For it is right by the sea, and surrounded by the sea on all sides; and there is no other way into it, except that provided by a narrow rocky passage – and there, three armed warriors could forbid all entry, even if you took up your stand with the whole of Britain behind you.' (**Colour plate 6.**)

This *angusta rupes*, confined crag or narrow passage, will be returned to in a moment. The rest of the story has first to be told. The wizard Merlin is summoned, and provides a solution. Uther will be magically changed into the likeness of Gorlois, Ulfin and Merlin into that of two of Gorlois's companions. At dusk this outwardly-transformed band of three arrives at Tintagel, and is admitted by the guards – 'and so' Geoffrey explains 'in that night was the

13 *The medieval approach to Tintagel Castle, a path down a hollow way, now overgrown and forgotten* (photo: author).

most famous of men, Arthur, conceived'. Meanwhile, back at Dimilioc Duke Gorlois most unwisely sallies forth to meet a challenge and is slain. Some of his men escape, cross the countryside to Tintagel and nerve themselves to break the awful news to Igerna. To their astonishment they see one whom they take to be Gorlois in person, sitting and smiling beside her. King Uther (for it is he, in the guise of the fallen duke) leaves, on pretence of making peace with himself, though when he reaches the fallen Dimilioc the magic has worn off and he is to be seen again as his true self. Later, he returns to Tintagel; later still, he weds the widowed Igerna; and two children are born to them, Arthur and his sister Anna.

A strict reading of Geoffrey's *History* allows the conception by trickery of Arthur, at Tintagel; and the occupation of Tintagel as a maritime fortress by Gorlois of Cornwall. That is all. The *History* nowhere claims that Arthur was born at Tintagel, or that he ever visited the place in later life, or that in any sense the stronghold became his property when he was king. Indeed at a later stage when Arthur, as ruler of Britain, is campaigning on the Continent we meet among his war-leaders and nobility Cador, duke of Cornwall – a successor to Gorlois – and in a list of those lost during a battle, the name of Aliduc *de Tintagol*, perhaps

meant to have been the castle's occupant. On so slight a foundation, almost every subsequent writer was able to expand the conception of Arthur at Tintagel to his birth there and, by implication, ownership and even residency.

The true significance of what Ulfin is made to say to Uther about the way in to Tintagel can only be appreciated on the spot, which is why it seems fair to assume that Geoffrey of Monmouth had been there. A trackway winds northward, from west of Tintagel village, past the vicarage and along the western crest of the valley; then it becomes a hollow way for the last fifty yards or so, and ends outside the once-arched gateway to the Lower Ward of Richard's thirteenth-century castle (**13**). This is the medieval approach, down which rode men and women on stubby little ponies, swatting at flies and brushing aside the brambles. Very few people today either use it or know about it. But the last short stretch, in front of the Lower Ward entrance, is along a flat shelf of rocky path, its left side the face of the high crag on which sits the Upper Ward, its right side falling away sharply into the upper end of the Great Ditch (**14**). The stretch is not as narrow now as it was in the Middle Ages because it has been widened and revetted to ease access for visitors. If Gorlois came back to life, he would need seven or eight men, not three, to hold the path against Uther's army.

If the ditch, a huge excavated feature, were not there, the path would be crossing a slight slope, but would in no sense be restricted.

Therefore, in the 1130s, whether Geoffrey was there himself or whether somebody managed to give him a full and accurate word-picture, the Great Ditch *was* there already. And because

14 *The final entrance to the Lower Ward. Sarah, an English Heritage custodian, demonstrates just where 'the three armed warriors could forbid all entry'* (photo: author).

15 *The Upper and Lower, landward, Wards of the Castle from the east. The southern* (left, in the picture) *outer wall of the Lower Ward surmounts the original inner rampart bank of the Great Ditch, here seen outside it* (photo: RCHME).

the spoil, or upcast, from digging the ditch is mostly on the inner or seaward side of the defensive line, there must have been a rampart bank in place, with some kind of entry gap hard against the crag of the Upper Ward. But all this is being described, and inferred, a century before Earl Richard's Castle – and closer inspection confirms (p. 59) that the outer masonry curtain-wall of the Lower Ward does indeed stand on top of an earlier rampart bank (**15**). So, though we do not have to believe in Gorlois, or in his stronghold, we can believe that in the 1130s there was a ditch, with an inner bank, and an entrance of the width of three men. These are post-Roman, Period II, features. There are separate archaeological reasons (p. 58) for believing them to be of that early time, but Geoffrey's casual mention of the detail is an independent witness.

During the rest of the twelfth century Geoffrey's *History* became widely known. Copies circulated all over the place. What matters here is that Geoffrey provided the link between Tintagel and Arthur. As far as can be judged, the sequence is more or less direct from Geoffrey's short mention right up to the King Arthur's Castle Hotel of the 1890s and a King Arthur's Café in Fore Street, Tintagel, today (**16**). Popular imagination had been fired by this specific text. Over eight centuries, we can pick out glimpses at spaced intervals. During

16 *The legacy of Geoffrey of Monmouth; a typical sight in Tintagel of today* (photo: author).

the thirteenth century, for example, the chance that Richard Earl of Cornwall was inspired to build his eccentric castle because he had read Geoffrey of Monmouth has already been discussed. In certain later mentions of Tintagel, an alternation can be seen – when the castle itself is named – between the actual place-name (however spelled) and the descriptive title 'Arthur's' or 'King Arthur's', as if the two were generally recognized as meaning the same monument.

Later views of Tintagel

In 1478 William Worcestre (William of Worcester), travelling as a scholar-antiquary and making field-notes for his own use, visited Cornwall. He either saw, or found out about, a great many things. By his time Gorlois, as the husband of the mother of Arthur, had become muddled up with another imaginary earl of Cornwall, Cador. William was shown, as the location of Dimilioc, not St Dennis but the nearby and larger fort of Castle-an-Dinas. It is not certain that he went to Tintagel but he was informed about it. Geoffrey of Monmouth's link had become extended; *castrum de Tyntagelle* was the place where Arthur was both conceived *and* born. Some seventy years later, John Leland was travelling around in search of 'Englands Antiquitees' under the patronage of King Henry VIII. Leland did visit Tintagel and has left enough comment to give a useful picture of its physical condition at the time. Oddly, Leland's allusions to Arthur are confined to a brief mention in his notes on Glastonbury.

John Norden, born about the time (1549) that Leland was rounding off his itinerary, compiled a description of Cornwall in 1597 to 1604. Intended as part of a very much larger *Speculum Britanniae*, it was for various reasons not published – with its magnificent maps – until 1728. The relevant map (Hundred of Lesnewth – the hundreds were and are the old sub-divisions of Cornwall) features *Tintagell Castle, Trevena* for the village and *Tintagell* for the church. Norden's text, enlivened by a detailed side-view of the castle and Island (**17**), is descriptive but ends with 'Famous *Arthure* Kinge of the *Brytons* was here begotten in this castle by *Uter Pendragon*, upon Beautifull *Igerna*', which is taken from Geoffrey's *History*.

Richard Carew of Antony in east Cornwall (1555–1620) was the author of *The Survey of Cornwall* (1602). He may have been a patriotic Englishman but, where the past was involved, Carew wrote as a Cornishman identifying with the Britons, not the Saxons. Tintagel was only a long day's ride from Antony and he knew it well. His account of the Island – and note his use of the word 'our' – is simple enough. 'It is not laid up among the least vaunts of this castle, that *our* victorious Arthur was here begotten by the valiant Uther Pendragon upon the fair Igerna'. Carew is careful to add his own gloss on this; '– and that without taint of bastardy, saith Merlin, because her husband died some hours before'. We are then given a short poem, either by Carew or his brother-in-law William Carnsew:

> Tintogel in his ruines vauntes,
> > Sometime the seate of Kings,
> And place which worthy Arthur bred,
> > Whose prayse the Breton sings.

Here, 'the Breton' is Geoffrey of Monmouth, and the rest of the poem describes certain features on this Island (see Chapter 3).

During the seventeenth century the Arthurian ascription became firmly entrenched in maps and official sources. Joel Gascoyne's *A Map of the County of Cornwall Newly Surveyed* appeared in 1699; the first such large-scale map, nearly an inch to the mile, of any county. The main feature at Tintagel, by the Island, is *King Arthers Castle*. The Parliamentary Survey of Crown lands, in the wake of the civil war (1650), included all that had formed part of the Duchy of Cornwall. Charles Stewart, from

17 *John Norden's depiction of Tintagel (about 1600).*

1660 King Charles II, had in fact been Duke of Cornwall from his birth, 29 May 1630. The entry for the manor of Tintagel, the old manor of Bossiney acquired by Earl Richard four hundred years earlier, is long and of special interest because all the details would have been obtained locally. We are now entering modern times, physically, even if encumbered still with a legendary past. The sorry remnants of the castle are given as 'The Mannor or Mansion house commonly knowen by the name of King Arthur Castle alias Tintagell Castle'. Lands that went with it included King Arthur's Island, for which a grazing tenant John Billing was paying a small rent.

There is no point in ziz-zagging around a pile of eighteenth- and nineteenth-century topographical literature of Cornwall, in which any number of similar allusions can be found. In 1806 at the height of a boom in small-scale, almost Do-It-Yourself, mining ventures, a band of optimists obtained a Duchy sett or mining lease for the Island. They wanted to work it for galena (silver-lead), a common ore outcropping on the north Cornish coast from which very small amounts of silver can be extracted. This was advertised as 'The Wheal Heart Copper &

Lead Work. In King Arthur's Castle and Island etc in the parish of Tintagell'. The quest was economically hopeless, as was a later try in 1853 under the name of King Arthur Consols. In a third Duchy lease of the 1870s, when a more serious attempt was being financed, the adit (the horizontal tunnel for access and drainage) was said to be some 200 feet 'below the site of the supposed Great Hall of King Arthur'. If *supposed* is deleted and Earl Richard substituted for King Arthur, this is roughly correct. The catalogue for the sale of the Earl of Wharncliffe's estates in and around Tintagel, prepared in 1911 by Messrs J. Kittow & Son and a useful source (with all its maps) for local study, shows the most cautious wording in its photographically-illustrated Preface. 'The Estate is of exceptional interest from its romantic associations with the legends of King Arthur.' There wrote a professional businessman; no purchaser could possibly claim to have been misled.

This rapid sketch, from the 1130s to 1911, is intended to drive home a fact that is still either overlooked or deliberately ignored. There is no way in which we can tell what the inhabitants of the district in the early twelfth, or eleventh, or previous century really believed and told occasional visitors about Tintagel Island, but equally we have no reason to think that Arthur

– as a folk-memory of a supposed post-Roman British heroic leader, or as the aggrandized king of medieval writings – came into any of it. It seems far more likely that the site, focused on the dramatic nature of the Island, featured in Cornish belief as the one-time stronghold of ancient kings (unnamed) or possibly of the folkloristic King Mark. There are, elsewhere in Cornwall and Scilly, traces in place-names and in occasional early references of tales about Arthur, just as there are in most of Wales and southern Scotland, not to say other areas of southern England. But, given the nature of Geoffrey's *History of the Kings of Britain*, his clear tastes and his method of composition, we have to conclude that it was Geoffrey of Monmouth in the 1130s who decided to locate Arthur's magically-aided conception on Tintagel Island (or perhaps within the smaller mainland area beyond the Great Ditch). The entire body of subsequent references, sampled above, rests on this. There simply is no independently attested connection in early Cornish folklore locating Arthur, at any age or in any capacity, at Tintagel.

Archaeology and Tintagel

So much for the intangible past; what about its visible remnants? Archaeology, if we regard the digging up of antiquity as being the forerunner of controlled excavation, began in Cornwall with medieval episodes of opening tumuli, prehistoric burial-mounds, to search for buried treasure. It was resumed in earnest in the eighteenth century – barrows again being the favoured targets – in order to test intellectual ideas about the past. Not quite in the same category were assaults on disused buildings to plunder them for old timber or useful walling material. The latter can certainly be assumed for parts of Tintagel Castle, from the fourteenth century onward. However, no evidence has come to light to suggest that any form of excavation prompted by curiosity took place on the Island, or at least not on a detectable scale, until the nineteenth century. When this began, it did so for non-Arthurian reasons.

On the summit of the Island is a building, roofless but complete in plan, that was a thirteenth-century chapel or small church – it will be called 'the Chapel' here (**18**). When John Leland visited the place this chapel had not long ceased to be used for occasional worship; he was told that it was dedicated in honour of a saint whose name he gives as Ulette, Uliane and Juliana. There is no reason to doubt that, ever since the building was slightly modified after 1233 to serve as a detached chapel for the Castle, it bore this dedication. The Period III–Period IV history of the chapel is discussed later (p. 110). The patronal saint, supposedly a man, is recognized also at two fully parochial churches in the district. One is St Juliot, about a mile further north-east beyond Minster, better known as the church restored by Thomas Hardy. The other is the mother-church of Camelford – Lanteglos by Camelford (Cornish *nant eglos* 'Church Vale') 6 km (4 miles) south. At Lanteglos, the saint is known as Juliot or Julitta. At St Juliot, this appeared in Domesday Book as *Sanguiland*, representing *Sant* plus *Juiland*.

In 1855, three years after becoming Rector of Lanteglos, John James Wilkinson 'explored the interior' of the Island Chapel. He was an Oxford-educated parson with a general interest in church antiquities and a particular one in his own church and parish, and here he must have wanted to find out anything possible about his otherwise-unknown patron saint. Wilkinson, who was locally very popular and served on numerous occasions as Mayor of Camelford, was friendly with Richard Byrn Kinsman, the Cornish priest who from 1851 became Vicar of Tintagel. It looks as if Wilkinson's exploration took place with Kinsman's permission and support, though not necessarily at the latter's suggestion. The sole account of this pioneer excavation is a brief reference published in 1870. Wilkinson removed the rubbish, fallen stones and vegetation; cleared up the masonry altar-block; and drew attention to two large rectangular granite slabs (p. 112). The account then says that 'In the chancel' [the east end] were graves lined with slate, of no great depth. One of them contained some dark mould, but no bones.' He observed pieces of freestone, the local volcanic greenstone obtainable at the base of the Island, with Romanesque or Norman-period ornament. Wilkinson's note does not specify actual digging in 1855, but the slate-lined graves north and south of the altar-block had not previously been noticed or mentioned, nor it seems were they visible in 1870 when the diarist Francis Kilvert was on the Island and compiled a very full and accurate description. This raises the inference that Wilkinson *did* excavate, and then filled back. It is also likely

18 On Tintagel Island the thirteenth-century Chapel, as it was about 1890 (photo: Gibson, Penzance).

that he made a plan of the result of his work, in which case he would surely have given Kinsman a copy to put with the parish records at the Vicarage. This offers the best explanation for an otherwise unattributed plan (**19**), apparently showing Wilkinson's 1855 discoveries, which survives from the 1930s when H.M. Office of Works took over Tintagel Castle (and Island) as a guardianship monument.

19 Part of an H.M. Office of Works drawing (339/15, perhaps of 1938–9) of the Chapel, apparently including Wilkinson's 1855 graves at the east end (source: English Heritage, Historic Plans Room).

R.B. Kinsman, as Vicar, was the champion of both Castle and Island. He persuaded Prince Albert, who took a keen interest in the Duchy of Cornwall and was attempting to shift its administration from a late medieval to an early modern basis, to revive the office of Constable of the Castle of Tintagel. In this capacity, Kinsman (when not busy with other hobbies, like making stained glass) was constantly on site. He himself undertook a certain amount of work, with the aim of improving access for visitors, securing entry to the Island's Inner Ward by repairing the curtain-wall and building a new entrance, and trying to cope with the dangers of natural decay. The neck of land joining the mainland wards to the Island was falling away, on both sides – in 1840 part of the northern wall of the landward Lower Ward collapsed, with chunks of overhanging masonry to alarm nervous visitors. 'The gradual widening of the chasm is continually going on' Kinsman wrote in 1871 'and the fall of large portions of the cliff (especially on the northern part of the ruin) is frequently occurring.' Nevertheless Kinsman, who may have moved the odd worked stone around, refrained from any kind of archaeological digging. He was an acute observer, as his articles show, and a meticulous self-appointed custodian, and would have published any such excavation.

Other things were happening in the later nineteenth century. Tourism, eventually to eclipse metal mining as Cornwall's best-known industry, spread hand-in-hand with the new railway systems. John Murray's *Hand-Book* for Cornwall, the earliest and most prestigious of

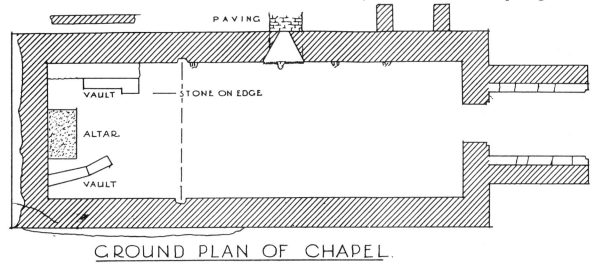

GROUND PLAN OF CHAPEL.

the county guides, came out in 1851. The descriptive text, which must have taken a year or more to compile, had been commissioned from T.C. Paris of Penzance, who seems to have travelled all around the county. A visit to Tintagel Castle was a must ('will be visited by every intelligent traveller') and we read of 'the ascent now presenting little difficulty, as a winding path has been cut in the face of the cliff'. This was a real stop-press item, as the new path with its steps was Kinsman's first project. The visitors would not normally have read Geoffrey of Monmouth, but increasingly they had been reading Tennyson's *Idylls of the King*, and may have known that the great man visited Tintagel in 1848, and did so again in 1860.

Hawker of Morwenstow, the Reverend Robert Stephen Hawker, spent his honeymoon (1823) at Tintagel 'in Lodgings for a Month – close to the Castle of King Arthur and amid the legends of his life and deeds', as he wrote to a friend forty years later. Hawker's long poem *The Quest of the Sangraal* (1863) was as important as Tennyson's verses in attracting the romantically-inclined to north Cornwall. Many others, in a list from Swinburne to Thomas Hardy, continued to find Tintagel poetically irresistible. If the picturesque, yet (thanks to Kinsman) accessible, ruins were attracting more and more visitors, limp volumes clutched in perspiring hands, we have to face the fact that feedback from these same tourists – who, unlike the locals, had been reading sheaves of this preparatory literature – quite clearly gave rise to new versions of old tales, and even new place-names. The little cove by the Island, the Haven or Porth Haven (p. 38), was always known as just that. By 1870 it had acquired a fresh name; Kilvert was informed by the aged guide, Mr Richards, that it was 'the King's Cove' or 'King Arthur's Cove'. The long sinuous cavern that penetrates the base of the Island and is flooded at high tide is mentioned, but with no label, from Carew's time (1603) until well into the nineteenth century. Under Tennysonian influence it became, as it is now, 'Merlin's Cave', and to judge from titles on old postcards this happened shortly before 1900. Paris, in Murray's *Hand-Book*, went far beyond Geoffrey of Monmouth's text in claiming that the Island was 'crowned with a ruinous castle of high antiquity, the reputed birthplace *and residence* of King Arthur' (added italics). Most locally-produced guidebooks copied this passage as if it were a well-known fact.

In 1918 a large chunk of clifftop ground on the Island outside, below and just east of the Inner Ward, collapsed; it all fell down to the beach, by the entrance to Merlin's Cave. This in itself was nothing new, but what happened next was unusual. William Taylor, builder and proprietor of the King Arthur's Castle Hotel and by now both a JP and the 'Mr Big' of Tintagel, noticed that there was some debris still overhanging. He sent men, who had to be lowered on ropes, to remove it; visitors to the Haven beach would have been in danger. The men reported that they had come across bones, sherds and portions of what looked like black wood. Further search was then made among the beach-boulders before high tides washed everything away.

Mr Taylor did all the right things. He marked the exact spot of the fall on a postcard (**20**) (the scar can still just be detected on the ground); he wrote an account; and, while informing the county museum, the Royal Institution of Cornwall at Truro, he sent specimen potsherds to the British Museum. The late Reginald Smith FSA wrote back that they were most probably Roman, and gave the curiously precise date of AD 50. Had it been realized that these were fragments of amphorae from the eastern Mediterranean, and of late fifth or early sixth century AD date, more interest might have been aroused. Two years previously, Reggie Smith had positively identified some locally-made, post-Roman, grass-marked pottery from west Cornwall as 'certainly of the Neolithic Age'; with Taylor's pieces, he was at least in the right millennium. After the First World War, William Taylor gave ten of the most interesting-looking sherds to the Royal Institution of Cornwall, together with part of a human jaw and some adult teeth, from their condition not perhaps of any great age. In 1933 his daughter Mrs Woolnough presented the rest of the collection, a further 46 Period II sherds. The RIC preserves a detailed file with all the papers.

It remains to add that, in the 1988 cataloguing of all the Tintagel finds, the 1918 Cliff Fall batch proved to be of very particular interest; it was from the lower contents of an extensive midden-spread, due to erosion sited on the cliff edge, and it can now be explained what it was doing there (p. 121).

POSITION OF 1918 CLIFF FALL.

20 *Postcard view of Tintagel Island, 1918, on which Mr William Taylor has indicated the position of the 'Cliff Fall'.*

A tourist Tintagel

William Taylor's own little *History of Tintagel* (1927) is a workmanlike account with a great deal of useful information. What it hints at, but does not say, is that in the later part of the author's lifetime the stage was being set for a very different sort of Tintagel – one where the formal, official, excavations of 1933–8 described in Chapter 4 might have been seen as a likely next step. The picturesque and straggling hamlet of Trevena (**21**), as visited by Tennyson, Wilkie Collins, Dinah Mulock Craik, Thomas Hardy with his first wife Emma, and a host of other chroniclers was fast disappearing. So, too, was the local economic mainstay, the dangerous industry of quarrying the sea-cliffs for slate. The local reaction to the 1895 acquisition by the National Trust of Barras Nose, the little headland on the eastern side of Tintagel Cove, is not recorded. On the other hand, it could be pointed out that this at once blocked any seaward extension of William Taylor's hotel, plans for which slightly preceded the purchase. By 1927 there were would-be developers in and around Tintagel who, realizing that the future lay with tourism – for preference, nice middle-class English visitors with money, spending most days out of doors – saw every reason to follow Taylor's example. If they could not find a piece of cliff to put up another jumbo hotel, they could erect bungalows. Unselective development became an immediate threat, and it is only necessary to look at the kind of bungalows still (1992) being permitted by the local auth-

ority, North Cornwall District Council, to shudder at what might have been in the pre-planning age. A Tintagel Cliff Preservation Fund was formed. It staged a money-raising Arthurian pageant at the Vicarage garden in 1930, and raised enough to allow the National Trust to buy a crucial 56 acres of Glebe Cliff, the stretch between the Castle and the parish churchyard. Anyone who experiences, from this wild tract, the unforgettable view of the Island in winter gales or a midsummer evening must be profoundly grateful to the Cliff Preservation visionaries.

Meanwhile the Island and the Castle were still there, coming into State care in 1929–30; still a magnet for visitors; still framed in the great windows of Taylor's hotel, where Elgar was moved to complete his Second Symphony, and Mary Ellen Chase to write her *Dawn in Lyonesse* (Macmillan, N.Y. 1938), a novel actually set in the hotel. All the literature of the period between the two World Wars was, for the locality, still completely Arthurian in tone. The Great Western Railway's range of inspired publications, engaging such writers as M.R. James and S.P.B. Mais, brought the medium-spenders to Cornwall in droves. R.B. Kinsman, vicar and last Constable, had died in the 1890s and eventually the access to the Island ceased to involve all the hassle of getting a key from Florence Nightingale Richards, the aged and mustachioed guardian of the ruins. The roof of the old mill-house, half-way down the valley (**22**) and once the Richards' home, collapsed. From time to time, greenery-yallery young men in Oxford bags got into the Castle at night and played their banjoes or ukuleles to the moon.

But what precisely were all these ruins? Elsewhere, comparable monuments like the larger abbeys did have a modicum of notices on site, sixpenny leaflets and interpretative aids. Post-Kinsman guidebooks to the district, hearty in their approach but pretty weak when it came to historical facts, continued to play the Arthurian card. The last of the pure nineteenth-century Arthurianists was yet another vicar, W.J.C. Armstrong at Boscastle. By 1930 Mr Armstrong's hearty little booklets – each appropriately issued as *A Rambler's Guide To* – told you all that you wanted to know as you strode along, knapsack on back, pipe in mouth, wind in your hair.

A sample 'One Minute Biography' for the

Trevena, Tintagel, from a sketch by the Author in 1862. [Fig. 1]

22 (Above) *The valley approach to Tintagel Castle (the Upper and Lower Wards are visible, top left).* (Right, foreground) *The old Mill House* (photo: Francis Frith & Co.).

rambler reads as follows:

> Who? King Arthur.
> Where? England.
> When? Fifth to Sixth Centuries.
> Why Famous? A national hero of Britain.

However, as more and more people came to sunny Cornwall, in more and more little cars packed with dogs, shrimping nets and inquisitive children, grey old Tintagel proved insufficient as it stood. As the first of a new line of

21 (Left, above and below) *'The picturesque and straggling hamlet of Trevena'.* (Top) *sketch of Fore Street in 1862 – note the parish church on the skyline – by Sir John Maclean.* (Below) *the Old Post Office (now a National Trust property) the only surviving late-medieval house in the village, taken about 1890* (photo: Gibson, Penzance).

guidebooks put it, 'With the growing interest, a fuller investigation of the remains was required'. Readers of the *Daily Mail* knew that in South Wales, at Caerleon, R.E.M. (later Sir Mortimer) Wheeler had got £1000 out of that paper, ostensibly to find King Arthur's Round Table but in fact to uncover the Roman fortress.

The Office of Works Tintagel excavations that began, as can now be seen, inevitably, in 1933 must occupy a chapter to themselves. Before that, the reader deserves an abbreviated Rambler's Guide on paper, pointing out all the various features of interest on the Island. Most of them have a history and mythology of their own, and a discussion can provide a helpful setting for the tale of the 1933–8 archaeological campaign. And before *that*, it would be a pity to end the present chapter without taking note of one significant event that most assuredly cannot be overlooked. Around 1920, Frederick Thomas Glasscock the reputed millionaire (of 'Monk and Glass' custard-powder fame) retired to Tintagel with his wife and built a new home there. One day, he happened to glance into a shop window. What was revealed to him, and what were the colourful repercussions of that revelation, will be examined sympathetically in our final chapter.

33

3

'Stepped at one stride across the sea . . .'

Though the top of Tintagel Island, at an average of 60m (190 ft) above mean sea level, is often called 'a plateau' it is misleading to think of it as a table. It is shaped more like a loaf with an undulating surface, the lower parts of all its sides being nearly vertical and rocky, but the upper angles shaved off to form steep grassy slopes. There is hardly a spot where anyone could fall off the edge into the boiling seas below, and no memory of anyone ever having done so. Sheep, of a small unimproved West Country breed, grazed on the Island for centuries after the Castle fell into disuse. A famous photograph (**23**) showing them (plus feeding-crib) inside the Inner Ward was taken about 1900 by Alex Old of Wadebridge, but it was then sold on to larger postcard firms like Frith's and misleadingly appeared until the 1940s. Many large archaeological monuments in Queen Victoria's reign were grazed by sheep, or goats, or in the mining districts of Cornwall by donkeys, who obligingly ate down the gorse bushes. This explains why, for the Island, Sir John Maclean's plan – drawn for him in 1870 by the Revd William Iago – shows as dotted lines the rectilinear traces of buildings and foundations around the Chapel, Radford's Site A (**24**). By 1930, these and other traces of Period II (or IV) remains on the Island were cloaked by a tussocky growth of grass and sea-pinks (as they are today). In the sheep-grazing era, they probably showed as the tops of walling. Unfortunately 1870 was also too early for any notion of making a complete, accurate, survey of everything detectable.

The official (Ordnance Survey) name of the Island is Tintagel *Head* (though both this and 'The Island' are given on current maps). Because to shipping it is partly a landmark, 'Tintagel Head' is also found in, for example, the *West Coast of England Pilot* (10th edn. 1960). An earlier name, again reflecting what could be seen from the sea, was Black Head. Iago's 1870 map drawn for Maclean, which is stated to be from an older one (about 1846) by Henry McLauchlan, marks 'Tintagel Head' for the south-west corner of the Island, but also 'Pen Diu' by the north-west corner. On the face of it, this looks like Cornish *pen* 'head, end, promontory' and *du* 'black'. Far from being a survival from local terminology in Period IV, III or even II it appears to be a retrospective translation by someone who thought that a Cornish form of 'Black Head' ought to exist. The culprit was William Hals (1655–1737), a most inventive writer in whose partly-published *Parochial History of Cornwall* (1750) fact and fiction are mingled like maypole ribbons. Hals was also responsible for the idea that Tintagel appears in Domesday Book as *Duns-cheine*, or *Dune-cheine*, which he managed to explain as the fortress (*dun*) approached by 'an Iron *Chain* and Draw-Bridge' – the truth is that he picked out, at a guess, the Domesday place-name *Donecheniv* which is now Downinney in Warbstow parish.

23 *'Sheep May Safely Graze' (as indeed they did, for centuries). The best-known of all the early Tintagel postcards, taken about 1900 (photo: Alex Old, Wadebridge).*

24 *Sir John Maclean's plan of part of the Island, 1870. Note traces of foundations (Site A) by the Chapel and, top left, an arrow with 'In a ravine beyond, is a well, half way down to the sea'.*

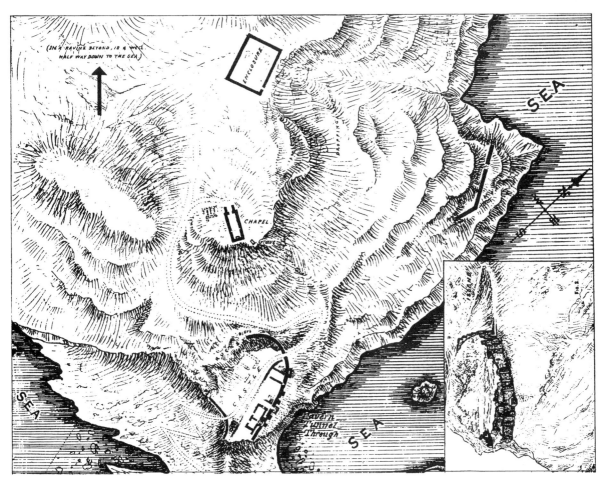

25 *The Neck, a 'V-shaped gulf'* (photo: RCHME).

This is mentioned, because the fictitious 'Pendiu' and 'Dun-chain' still sneak their way into local pamphlets. In 1602 Richard Carew knew only of 'the fardest poynt of this hill . . ., called Black Head, well knowne to the coasting Mariners'.

Access by land

The Island is separated from the mainland, and consequently the Castle's Inner Ward from the two landward-side (Upper and Lower) Wards, by an unstable chasm or neck (**25**). In all early representations, like John Norden's of around 1600 showing a V-shaped gulf marked *ye Descent & ye Ascent*, this is further characterized by narrow winding paths with sharp angles. There are Victorian accounts in which timid visitors took one look and never made it to the Island at all. Richard Byrn Kinsman in 1851 improved 'ye Ascent' by getting quarrymen to cut new steps, and this access, with minor diversions, served well enough until the 1970s when the crumbling sides of the chasm had to be grouted and stabilized, and a long wooden bridge was flung across the neck or ridge at the base of the divide.

This is not a plea to would-be visitors to see

the Island now, before a chair-lift becomes essential (though at some future date even the present access may collapse). Visitors ask two simple questions; 'How long before this becomes a real island?' and 'How did they get up there in the olden days when the Castle was occupied?' One way to answer both is to stand on the plateau and look north-eastward along the coast (**colour plate 2**). Barras Nose, the smaller headland on the east side of the Haven, gives some idea of what Tintagel as a promontory may have resembled two or three thousand years ago. A mile or so further is the larger headland of Willapark; and right offshore a dark rocky mass, a multiple-island called The Sisters. This, in its turn, offers some notion of what Tintagel may resemble two or three thousand years ahead.

Geologists whose operational timescale covers hundreds of millions of years can be remarkably patient with archaeologists who tend to think in terms of centuries. Nor can any one geologist be fairly expected to be pinned down to a firm conclusion about some natural feature that is no longer there. An informed (geological) opinion, however, is that the Tintagel Island–Barras Nose–Sisters demonstration is a rough but fair one and that, given the complex nature of the Island's visible geology, continued and sometimes rapid erosion, since Roman and post-Roman times, has taken place of what may once really have looked more like Barras Nose – a not too narrow grassy saddle linking mainland and Island, and at a height considerably above that of the present wooden bridge.

Whether, in (say) the fifth and sixth centuries AD, it was ever possible to clamber up the side of such a saddle from the Haven we cannot tell; but the presence of the Great Ditch, if it is of this date, rather implies that the perceived point of any attack was from the landward angle. Moving onward to Period IV and the thirteenth century, by which date further erosion of the supposed saddle would have taken place, it is notable that Richard's Castle was from the start in two distinct parts: Island and landward. Since the landward Lower Ward's walling was carried around its *northern* side, and that of the Inner Ward almost certainly around its *southern* side outside the Great Hall (p. 120), both parts were fully guarded against the area of any saddle or neck between them. Much more than this cannot be said, because any defensive aspects on the saddle itself have long ago vanished.

The rocks below the Iron Gate (p. 41) as a landing-stage have their own story, but the fact that this landing was fortified in Period IV must suggest that, inconvenient as it may have been for manhandling heavy goods to the Island's top, the pathway up was preferable to using any sort of zigzag ascent from the Haven up the eastern flank of the neck. The question of when, and at what rate, and to what extent, the neck had fallen away by the fourteenth and fifteenth centuries introduces another topic where a little too much may have been read into early remarks.

The drawbridge
Around 1600 John Norden wrote that 'a Draw-Bridge was lett downe to pass to the Ilande to the other buyldinges; but of late years, *within mans memorie*, it is depryved of that benefite of a bridge.' In these extracts, the crucial words will be italicized for emphasis. Richard Carew (publishing in 1602) has: 'Halfe the buildings were raysed on the continent, and the other halfe on an Iland, continued together (*within mens remembrance*) by a drawe bridge, but now divorced, by the downefalne steepe Cliffes.' This may be independent, but Carew and Norden are saying much the same. Neither of them actually *saw* any drawbridge. What did John Leland see, going back sixty years before this? He commented that both the Inner and the Lower Wards '. . . be woren away with gulfying yn of the se, yn so much that yt hath made ther almost an isle' and he observed that 'and no way ys to go ynto hyt [the Island] now but by *longe elme trees* layde for a bryge.'

This is a very different matter. It means that by the end of the fifteenth century, when the Castle was in considerable decay anyhow – William Worcestre (1478) had been told that *castrum Tyntagelle*, where Arthur had been conceived, was *dirutum* 'in ruins' – the neck had fallen away to the point where a rough bridge of tree-trunks had to be laid across. A fixed access of this kind is not the same as a proper drawbridge with framing, chains and a windlass. And fuller scrutiny of what people wrote, after Leland, confirms that the 'drawbridge' claim was never more than a story. Sir Richard Grenville (p. 41) in 1583 inspected the whole place. 'From the utter great gate on the maine [i.e. the now-vanished north-wall

gateway of the Lower Ward] ther hath ben, *within the memorie of some that dwell thereby*, a drawbridge, which is now gon' and his plan has '*the place whair the drawe bridge was*'.

The tentative conclusion has to be that no credible witness ever saw a genuine, medieval-style, drawbridge; all knew that there had been some kind of bridge before the middle of the sixteenth century, but this was an informal affair of tree-trunks or planks laid across. Carew's (or William Carnsew's) little poem sums it up:

> A bridge these buildings ioynd, whom now
> The fallen cliffs diuorce . . .

The place-name
Tintagel is one of many instances in Cornwall where the locality, the features found or constructed in it, and eventually the whole parish, is named for a single, and the most striking, aspect – in this case the Island and its mainland root. The name was always difficult to explain, partly because scholars were not sure what language it was in – Norman French, for instance? – but there has been a general supposition that first part is Cornish *din-* (which does occur as *tin-*) meaning not only 'fortress, hillfort, ancient stronghold' but also 'natural stronghold, place resembling a fortress'. Oliver Padel's recent explanation is the most convincing. The second part may be a Cornish word *tagell* (assumed to have existed because of Welsh *tagell* 'jowl' and Breton *tagell* 'collar, snare'), from the Cornish verbal root *tage* 'choke'. It would therefore mean something like 'constriction', and would be a good description of the Island's neck. *Tagell* would have a hard /g/ (rhymes with 'snaggle'), and we have to guess that early writers in Norman French and Latin, like the poet Beroul and Geoffrey of Monmouth, saw this in *writing*. When *spoken* in Norman French, this *g* became a /j/ sound, hence in 1207 the name of Robert de *Tintaioel* (where the second *i* represents /j/, or very close to it) and Geoffrey's own *Tintagol* (with *g* = /j/), which because of the prestige of these literary forms the present pronunciation.

Access by sea
Visitors in midwinter, when giant Atlantic waves pound the Island and the cliffs, and the valley's streamwater normally cascading down on to the top of the beach can all be blown upwards as spray before ever reaching the

26 *Tintagel Haven on a sunny day – 'the sea is blue and smooth'* (photo: author).

sand, should come back in midsummer (**26**). The sea is blue and smooth. The shingly beach gleams in the hot sun. Tiny children paddle in microscopic wavelets, dogs rush around, parents lean against the warm rocks and snooze. The proper name of the cove by the Island is The Haven, in itself suggestive of some former use by boats. (In east Cornwall's variety of spoken English dialect, the word *haven* was up to this century often pronounced 'hawn'. This gave rise, as we shall see (p. 43), to yet another invented place-name.)

Use of the Haven by coastal vessels of up to 100 tons burthen may still be just within the memories of those that live nearby, but the hard evidence is photographic (**27**). In the last century the Haven was the scene of no less than three industrial activities. The galena mine driven under the Island (p. 27) had a large waterpipe taking water from the valley, around the edge of the cove, to provide power from a wheel. There was also a staged timber walkway allowing the miners to reach the level way above the high-tide mark. Clearly visible in pre-1914 postcards and shown in paintings and drawings back to the 1860s, if not earlier, a series of slate-walled platforms with a capstan, derrick or poppet-head, planked lean-to's and small buildings, all at the head of the cove, served the owners of fishing boats which had to be lifted up and berthed where high seas could not reach them. It also functioned in another way, in the loading of large shipments of cut and graded slates brought down the valley track in carts (**28**). In good weather, trading coasters came up on the beach at high water and were made fast. Batches of slates were swung out and down, even taken the short way to the ships with a little trolley on rails, and then swung aboard, the vessels departing at the next high tide.

There is no firm evidence as to how far back this usage went, but the inshore fishing was probably the oldest industry. An official muster of 1626 lists mariners and fishermen (the two are distinguished) from all around Devon and Cornwall. Thirteen men at Tintagel are named as mariners, perhaps employed on larger ships at Boscastle where in 1629 there were four barques from 25 to 30 tons. Under Tintagel parish, 'Sailors and Fishermen did not appear', but this does not necessarily mean that fishermen did not exist.

27 (Above) *A hive of industry: Tintagel Haven in the late nineteenth century, with derricks and capstans, a coastal trading-ship and, against the Island, the walk-way and levels of the King Arthur Mine* (photo: S. Thorn, Bude).

28 (Left) *The Haven, about 1905, with the timber gantries and lifts used to load slate and raise small boats; note also the precipitous path to the neck and, with a rope, up to the Island* (photo: Martin, N. Devon).

Despite the occasional scepticism of archaeologists, or of those who do not know Tintagel properly all the year around, there can be no doubt at all that during the entire period AD – certainly during Periods II, III and IV – the Island was fully accessible by sea. The main variable has been the relative heights of mean sea level (MSL). Taking now, or AD 2000, as a time datum, MSL in AD 1300 would have been about 1.5 m (5 ft) lower, and in AD 500 about 3.35 m (11 ft) lower (approximately calculated).

The beach of Tintagel Haven was not invariably a safe landing. William Taylor, whose

hotel provided a grandstand seat for such happenings, commented gloomily (1927) that 'it was not an uncommon occurrence for a small trading boat to load with slate on the beach during the day, and with a rising tide and ground swell to be smashed in pieces before getting afloat'. There was, however, an alternative method of landing (**29**). The feature known as the Iron Gate is a more or less level, stepped, platform of rock surface at the eastern base of the Island, jutting out slightly into the Haven. A short steep grass bank above it, with traces of a once rock-cut path, leads up to a defensive work of the thirteenth century, through which a large doorway gives access to the steep but direct pathway going obliquely up the side of the Island to the Inner Ward.

The Iron Gate is in fact a natural quay. At low water, standing on it, the face of the rock shelf can be seen falling almost vertically down into deep water (**30**). The outer part of the cove, below low-water mark, is fairly deep. In 1583, Sir Richard Grenville's plan states that below 'the rockes to lande men on to of sheipes [and he was concerned that the 'sheipes' might be those of foreign foes] the baye is all fayer sandy grounde good to ancor in and there is never lesse than five fathom [= 9 m (30 ft)] of water at the loest ebbe, shepes may ryed there all wyndes except the north west.' What was true in the sixteenth century would have been so in the thirteenth. Grenville saw the Iron Gate rocks as a quay, where 'the greatest sortes of shippes' could perhaps 'lay their sides to the workes, and land ani companie of men' (**31** and **colour plate 7**).

The context of Grenville's report was the threat of Spanish invasion. Sir Richard was a Cornishman, a considerable hero with his Great House at Stow, further up the coast. The view of the Cornish as visionary, sentimental Celts is for external consumption only; Cornwall has produced far more than its expected quotient of inventors, entrepreneurs and smart commercial operators. What Sir Richard reported to the Council of State was one matter;

30 *A view (inland) along the near-vertical frontage of the Iron Gate rocks, as a natural wharf* (photo: Susanna Thomas).

29 *(Top) The Iron Gate landing; the rocky platform and the medieval defensive wall above it, seen from Barras Nose. (Below) Defences from inside and above; note the walkway along the top of the main wall, and (lower right) a smaller stretch added in the fourteenth century* (photos: RCHME).

what, having looked closely at Tintagel Haven, he may have suggested to his friends and compatriots is quite another. Here was a potential deep-water inlet that seemed to have been overlooked. There exists a unique copy of Richard Carew's 1602 *Survey*, a kind of proof version marked up by the author for his projected, but unrealized, revised edition. Against the poem about Tintagel, Carew wrote in the margin:

The late worthy gent: Grayvile [Grenville, also spelled Grey(n)vile] went about a very comendable work here to have made a kay [quay] the place so commodious apt ynough & ev'y way to ben behoofull [behoveful, or useful] as great pitty none now endevour to perform the same etc.

31 *Sir Richard Grenville's 1583 plan.* 1 '*a cave*'; 2 '*the chapel*'; 3 '*a garden walled*'; 4 '*a fayer sprynge of water*'; 5 '*a place to land at*'; 6 '*A, B, 2 Rampiers to defend the landing*'; 7 '*the wailles of the Iron Gate*'.

It was an idea, a venture on his own account; it is dubious as to whether it would have worked.

As for the actual Iron Gate, presumably in the doorway of the defence-work, this may be in the same situation as the drawbridge. Apart from the improbability of an all-iron door in the thirteenth century (and of what kind: wrought iron? cast iron? hammer-rivetted plates?), no one ever saw it. Leland has 'men alyve saw ther yn a postern dore of yren', Norden wrote of 'garretted wall yet in parte remayninge, where-in was a gate of Iron, which gate is now removed'. The answer may be not archaeological at all, but linguistic. The Cornish language had two identical words *porth*. One (Latin *portus*) included the senses 'harbour, cove, landing-place'. This is very common in coastal names and outlasted the demise of spoken Cornish to become a dialect word (porth, por, par) in both Cornwall and Scilly. The other, from Latin *porta*, meant a doorway, gateway, entrance and hence like French *porte* an actual door. At Tintagel, a medieval composite place-name Porth Hawn, with Cornish-into-English *porth* 'landing-place' and dialect *hawn* for 'haven' is not attested but is quite likely. The Cornish for 'iron' is *horn*, older *hoern*. 'Iron Gate' would be *porth horn*, close enough even with its slight /r/ sound to Porth Hawn. The chance that people who knew some Cornish (like Carew) confused the one with the other is strong, and a gate of iron was deduced from the muddle. In fact this is indicated in the seventeenth century account by William Hals who, liar and forger though he may have been, knew a lot of Cornish. Hals talks of the long, lofty and strong wall 'through which was a gate, callen in British Porth Horne, Anglice Iron Gate'.

The defensive wall, with its narrow walkway and battlement, is of the same character and date as the Castle. A fortified landing here implies that the landing was used. Down on the rocks, near the edge of this natural wharf, are two deep square hollows cut into the slate (**32**) which must have been to seat square-based timber mooring posts, or a simple jib for unloading, or both. Around the rock shelf, northward, there is a sea-filled gully leading into a long cavern, going back under the island. There are a dozen or so ancient, worn rock-cut steps here down to a slippery shelf, and further in are remains of an undated masonry wall. As with the spur running out from Barras Nose into the Haven, geologically this point is at the base of the slate strata constituting the Island and getting to the volcanic greenstone, used in the Castle for the detailing of door and window surrounds, coigns, jambs etc. The natural cave, with the steps, may be one of several thirteenth-century quarrying points.

In the 1933–8 excavations, the area inside the Iron Gate wall, with the shorter stretch of later battlemented wall by its southern end, was tidied up rather then excavated. Pieces of only three identifiable medieval pots were found (there is no suggestion, of course, that this entrance-area was inhabited). During the post-Roman period, mean sea level (in AD 500, say) at 3.35 m (11 ft) lower than now would still have made it possible, and in still conditions quite safe, for a sea-going ship to have been tied up (with fenders) against the rock face. There is in fact much in favour of the claim that the Iron Gate Rocks formed the post-Roman landing place from which ship-borne goods entered the citadel. In the 1930s clearance, about a dozen sherds of post-Roman imported pottery were picked up inside the Iron Gate wall. In recent years, with careful search, more like eighty such sherds have been recovered, mostly on or besides the lower part of the pathway to the top. An explanation that these result from long-term downhill slippage of debris from the top will not do – the distance is far too great. The other explanation would be that these bits represent occasional breakage in handling and in transit. It cannot, by its nature, be proved that this was a natural post-Roman wharf; but it might well be thought that early shipmasters from afar, used to the real quays of places like Alexandria and Rhodes, preferred to stay afloat standing off from a platform, rather than to risk their only means of return on an uncertain beach.

Sustenance

In earlier times (and this includes the 1930s) the suitability of Tintagel Island for more or less permanent occupation was never questioned. This is a trap into which topographical writers, even archaeologists, who have not been there in midwinter can still fall. North-westerly gales force the spray right over the Island; it is piercingly chilly; only in the natural hollow occupied by the Inner Ward, and then solely when behind stout walls, would life be tolerable. At the completely exposed Site D, once seriously put forward as the remains of

farm buildings, one might as well be on a Greenland ice-floe. 'Summer visitors, under the placid surroundings, have little idea of what a winter at Tintagel can be' was William Taylor's fair warning. 'After a north-west gale the herbage for miles inland is quite salt to the taste, and the grass turns a red hue.'

The total area of the Island (flat on a map) is 11 ha (27 acres), and of the summit about 4.5 ha (11 acres). In all the centuries of sheep-grazing, the maximum for stock was held to be thirty beasts, a round figure still remembered. Fresh water was essential. There is a romantic belief that water from far inland in some fashion percolates below the neck, and wells upward to the summit. This is, hydrologically speaking, moonshine. The aquifer is dependent solely on annual rainfall. It can vary considerably. There is a just-detectable depression running across the plateau, of which the walled Garden (p. 47) takes advantage (33). The principal watering-point is the well (33, no. 2), rock-cut and lined with masonry. It is known to be about 5 m (16 ft) deep, can be pumped dry in a day, and when cleaned out in the 1930s produced a few medieval sherds. There is no water access in the Inner Ward – a small rock-cut cistern, cleared out in 1988, was either a soakaway or an inefficient rainwater collector – and the lined well can be assigned to the thirteenth-century Castle. The so-called 'rock basin' near it (no. 1) is a small hollow probably hacked out for the benefit of sheep, and of no great age.

The depression is drained at its east end by a spring, in a little hollow (no. 3). The water runs under the turf down the slope between Sites C and B, where there is a neat little basin surrounded by placed stones, possibly medieval (no. 4). These features hold water for most of the year, and were noticed in the past. Richard Carew's poem has:

A Spring there wets his head, his foote
A gate of Iron gardes

where 'he' is the Island. Leland, and in 1583 the man of action Grenville, both noticed either this spring or the well. At the south-west end of the depression (no. 5), moisture seeps out from

32 (Top) *The northern rock-cut square hollow on the Iron Gate rocks, filled with water* (photo: author). (Below) *Detail of the same, emptied* (photo: RCHME).

below the rock, and excavation here would probably establish a further spring. More interesting is no. 6. This is far down the grassy slope on the north-west flank of the Island. A small platform has been scooped out, and at its back is the water, in a hollow with signs of a built stone surround. One of Sir John Maclean's 1870 plans (see **24**) has an arrow with 'In a ravine beyond is a well, half way down to the sea'. The age of this catchment is unknown, but again perhaps medieval.

As far as can be ascertained from fieldwork, these are all the sources of water. Not one begins to match, in volume, the flow of the stream down the landward-side valley, but at least they are on the Island and most of them survive even a summer of drought. While there could never have been enough water for a large permanent population of men and beasts, with careful use (supplemented by laborious fetchings of water from the valley) the supply should have sufficed for temporary occupation.

Exploitation for food production, in any sense, is less easy to show. The rectangular walled Garden (**34**), somewhat restored, figures in most early accounts. It could have been enclosed at any date between the 1230s and the fifteenth century. The outcome of the 1930s work here was the discovery that its northern corner sits above the foundations of (presumably) post-Roman structures. It is an attractive feature – in recent times, custodians have thoughtfully introduced bluebells – and it deserves some attention from the garden-history movement. Because it is only some 50 m (160 ft) from the Chapel, the Garden has sometimes been taken to be a graveyard. This is found as late as Kilvert's 1870 visit ('some distance further on from the chapel is the graveyard'). John Leland, however, with 'a grownd quadrant walled as yt were a garden plot', and Grenville 'a garden walled', would have been familiar with similar little herb-gardens in their own time.

The 1984–5 survey of the Island, by the Royal Commission on the Historical Monuments of England (RCHME), marks on the western side, within a sheltered patch of slope, a vestigial field-system of plots divided by paths. This was first spotted, in November sunshine when the grass was at its annual lowest, by Professor Etienne Rynne and the writer in the late 1970s. Again, we can but guess that this too is medieval and that since,

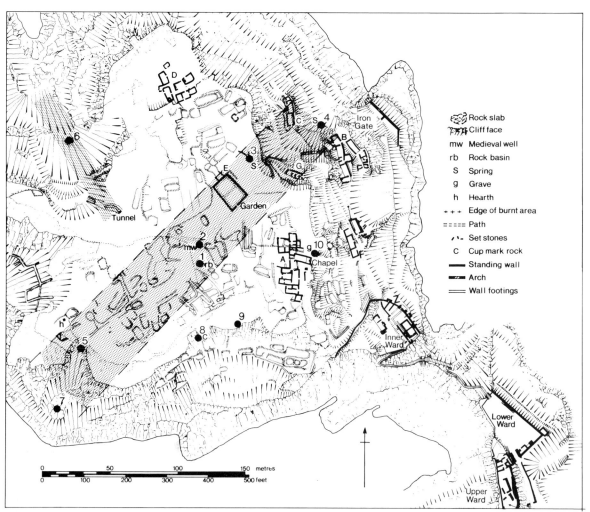

unlike the Garden, it is not protected from grazing livestock, it antedates the introduction of grazing in (probably) the fifteenth century.

The Tunnel

On the north-west part of the plateau, the Tunnel (35) like all such subterranean features invariably fascinates visitors, young and old. Except after heavy rain, it is possible to walk through it dryshod. It is more complicated than it looks. Clearance of the western or seaward end in the 1930s yielded no finds. Agreed facts are that the Tunnel has been rock-cut from the west; its eastern part comes through the surface, and must have been roofed; there are circular recesses at the western entrance for posts to frame a door; and the marks of cutting are those of small iron tools or dressing-picks of

33 *Tintagel Island: water sources and main 'folkloristic' features. Broken lines enclose the zone of main rainwater catchment. 1 rock basin. 2 medieval well; 3 spring; and 4 built shallow well, north-east side; 5 unexcavated spring, south-west side; and 6 built shallow well on the slope below the Tunnel; 7 Pinnacle Rock; 8 King Arthur's Seat, Window, Cups-and-Saucers; 9 King Arthur's Footprint; 10 King Arthur's Bed or Hip-Bath.*

medieval type. The internal profile, like a load-bearing arch, implies the work of medieval masons, probably those engaged in building the Castle. The floor, worn rock, slopes seaward so as to drain surface water (after rain) into the long slope where the spring-basin no. 6 can be

34 *The rectangular medieval walled herb-garden – the walls in part rebuilt – on the summit of the Island. The view is from the north-west, with Site A and the Chapel behind the Garden (*photo: RCHME*).*

found. Here and there, high up the sides, there seem to be shallow recesses as if to accommodate small cross-timbers (**36**).

It has never exactly been hidden. Early visitors all saw it. To Carew, it was 'a Cave, reaching once, by my guides report, some farre way under ground'. John Leland noticed just 'the ruines of a vault'. The tunnel was not in use, and one end was choked; Carew's poem has

> There, cave above, entrie admits
> But thorowfare denies.

Evidence for its pre-1600 date separates it from the much later cliff-mining ventures; mine levels were invariably cut man-height with an upright oval profile. New Age enthusiasts light upon this tunnel, as they do on most subterranean monuments of any age, as stone wombs for the enactment of symbolic rebirth, secret caverns employed for ordeals, or recesses where the credulous can experience shared dreams and enjoy the curative properties of radioactivity. Archaeologists, if and when they can be bothered to do so, counter such luxuriant thoughts with prosaic suggestions based on observed facts and likely analogies. One very prosaic idea is that the Tunnel is a detached larder or meat-store for the thirteenth-century Castle. Meat would have been hung from battens, cooled by a through-breeze and kept above the damp floor. One end had a closed door, and the other was covered by slate slabs and possibly a wooden grille. It is now known (but was not, until 1988) that it would have been impossible to have the usual kind of under-storey larder or foodstore below the Great Hall (p. 119). To object to this idea, on the grounds that the Tunnel is about an eighth of a mile from the Hall, is to impose modern values. A medieval head-cook or manciple would have been quite indifferent as to how many times a day a medieval scullion had to hump a side of salted beef back and forth.

The Arthurian features

In 1863 the scientist Robert Hunt (pioneer of photography, later Fellow of the Royal Society and a professor of mining geology) visited Tintagel to collect folklore. This pleasant pursuit had occupied many holidays; Hunt was a man with dozens of interests. He commented that the numerous tales from west Cornwall con-

35 *The Tunnel, showing rock-cut walls, 'arched' profile and sloping rock floor; a view through to the seaward (north-west) end. (The slab steps are modern)* (photo: RCHME).

36 *The Tunnel as a medieval larder? A helpful visitor indicates the positions of lateral beam-sockets* (photo: author).

cerning giants were, in the east of Cornwall, counterbalanced by similar legends in which King Arthur featured. However, 'the man who has charge of the castle', perhaps Edwin Richards, had no Arthur stories to tell to Hunt. It may just have been one of those days. It does go along with the fact that the detailed shilling guidebooks for tourists had only just started to appear. Nearly all overt Arthurian details first appear in print about 1870.

When the first official HMSO guidebook appeared in 1935, its author (C.A. Ralegh Radford) included this curt statement: 'No evidence whatsoever has been found to support the legendary connection of the Castle with King Arthur'. So grim, so plonking, a pronouncement from a government archaeologist should have ruled a thick black line across the page. It failed to do so. Rival and unofficial guides, published then (as now) by Tintagel shopkeepers, continued to plug an Arthurian past that was basically Tennysonian, with elements from secondary or tertiary versions of Geoffrey of Monmouth, even if obliged to accommodate some of the now-visible results of Radford's excavations.

Florence Nightingale Richards, last of the informants and key-holders who had worked under R.B. Kinsman as Constable, died after the First World War; her parents, Edwin and Sarah, had been born in the 1820s. It cannot be claimed that they (and still less Mr Kinsman) actually invented some of the folkloristic attributes on the Island, but there are no records earlier than this family's long spell as guides. Most famous of the exhibits was – still is – King Arthur's seat (**37**). It is marked, with its fellows, in the last of the location maps showing the quasi-archaeological features; that in one of Mr Armstrong's *Rambler's Guides*. The Seat is a natural notch in the slate cliff, just below the edge of the plateau on its southern side. A little slit within it is the Window. One can sit on the worn sloping floor, where there are some twenty small circular depressions 5 to 15 cm (2 to 6 in) across. Initials with dates (back to the seventeenth century, even) are cut among them. The earliest reference so far noticed was by Sabine Baring-Gould in an 1888 magazine article; '. . . where a smooth slab of slate has been thus scooped out into a succession of hollows, the people call them *King Arthur's cups and saucers*'. They are not quite like the prehistoric cup-marks (or cup-and-ring marks) of the Bronze Age, found in Britain and elsewhere in Cornwall. Chemical weathering, as Baring-Gould observed, can start such formations, even if these at Tintagel seem to have been deepened or emphasized by human handiwork (**colour plate 5**).

Just outside the Chapel, by its south-east corner, is something to which the names King Arthur's Bed, Elbow Chair and (collected locally, 1960s) Hip-Bath have all been given (**38**). It is an elongated east–west and slightly oval hollow, sides smoothed by exposure, cut down a few feet into the bedrock slate and obviously having lain open for centuries.

Shape, orientation and proximity to the Chapel suggest a medieval rock-cut grave, perhaps less likely to have been a chaplain's than the two encountered by Wilkinson within the Chapel in 1855. Leland saw it ('a pretty chapel with a tumbe on the left syde'). Carew thought it was 'an Hermites grave, hewen out in the rocke', and it may have attracted the same legend as the Welsh one attached to the grave of Amr in Herefordshire, which could never be measured as the same length twice and which altered its length to fit whatever size corpse was placed within it.

Between the Seat and the Chapel, on the highest point of the Island directly facing Glebe Cliff and the parish church, there is a smaller eroded hollow, the base of which has the shape of a large human footprint (**39**). This is King Arthur's Footstep (1872) or else his Footprint (1901, 1908), imprinted on the solid rock when he 'stepped at one stride across the sea to Tintagel Church!' (1889). Its dramatic exhibition to the wondering tourist, by Edwin Richards or his daughter Florence, was the highpoint of the guided tour. What further proof of Arthur's presence here could be asked for? The almost-forgotten Footprint, spurned these last sixty years in favour of straight archaeology, may be rather different from the other curiosities. It has significant parallels elsewhere. Arthur's or not, it may be genuinely Period II if not older, and will be fitted into a model of events proper to that time (p. 96).

There may have been other such Arthurian wonders. A tall jagged slate stack on the west side is now, tamely, just The Pinnacle; it was once flanked on the south by another which fell in the last century, known from its profile (a large nose detectable? a cocked hat?) as The Duke of Wellington. Because the lower sides of the Island are difficult if not dangerous to explore, there may be other nooks and crannies that once had names of their own. There are several caverns at sea-level, visible from a boat; that now called Merlin's Cave does indeed go right through the base of the Island, by the neck, from one side to the other.

Post-medieval defences?

Sir Richard Grenville in 1583 inspected Tintagel, among other places, in order to see if it offered a landing-point to an enemy and if so what could be done. Both his report and plan survive. The suggested recommendations for

37 (Top) *King Arthur's Seat, with the Cups-and-Saucers on the sloping floor; the slit is the Window* (photo: Susanna Thomas). (Left) *Detail of the cup-marks, improved in prehistoric or recent times* (photo: RCHME).

strengthening the place, costing about a hundred marks, were not accepted by the Council under Treasurer Burghley (William Cecil, first Lord Burghley), but one minor portion may have been carried out.

Grenville was apprehensive that enemy ships might try to put a raiding-party on to the rocks, and the slope, by the spring no. 6. It would be a hard task, even for today's Royal Marines. He wished to defend this with two little 'rampiers' – small blockhouses – which he marked as *a* and *b* on his plan. Rampier *b* has gone, but what seems to be its site, a small platform just over the edge, was picked up in

1985 in the RCHME survey. Rampier *a*, on the other hand, not only stood until 1817 or later, described as being 8 feet square with walls 6 feet high and a doorway flanked by window-spaces, it also then contained the rectangular slab of granite, 76 by 132 cm (30 by 52 in), that now forms the surface of the altar-block in the Chapel (p. 112). This almost certainly *was* an unconsecrated altar surface, brought to the Island in the thirteenth century, and it may have been purloined for the rampier as a hearth-stone. It bears no consecration crosses, nor inscription – only the irregularities of partially dressed granite. In 1817 it was thought to be the remains of an illegible epitaph for John de Northampton, Lord Mayor of London, who was exiled briefly to Tintagel in 1384/5 (but certainly did not die there). Kinsman, who

38 (Left) *King Arthur's Bed, Elbow Chair or Hip-Bath – a rock-cut east–west hollow by the Chapel, almost certainly a medieval grave* (photo: Susanna Thomas).

39 (Below) *King Arthur's Footprint – a hollow, shaped and improved by human agency, on the highest point of the Island's southern side* (photo: author).

40 *On the top of the Island, looking south-east across the plateau; foundations of Site D (rebuilt, in the 1930s) with (*right, foreground*), remains of Grenville's 1583 Rampier 'A' (*photo: RCHME).*

could well have recognized it as an altar component in the remains of the blockhouse, must have had it carried back to the Chapel, where in 1855 Wilkinson saw it.

It is just conceivable that, if the rampier was still 6 feet high in 1817, it had been repaired for use occasionally by a shepherd; and the subsequent removal of the wall-stones could simi-larly be explained by repairs to the Garden, if that were employed as a sheep-fold. In the 1930s Office of Works reconstructions, directed by a visiting architect and carried out by local labour, that followed each season of Radford's excavations, the foundations of the rampier were incorporated in the (highly improbable) reconstitution of the cluster called Site D, at one time displayed as the 'farm' of the 'Celtic monastery'. There it can be seen (**40**) – an isolated rectangular feature, meaningless as any of the larger cluster, Sir Richard's defensive work made real (but unrecognized until 1988). We can well doubt that this is the last of many surprises Tintagel Island still conceals.

4

Excavations in the 1930s

The most extensive excavation yet to take place at Tintagel started in 1933, on the Island, eventually including the Castle's mainland wards. The direction was entrusted by H.M. Office of Works to Courtenay Arthur Ralegh Radford, a Devon man as three of his four names indicate, from 1929 to 1934 an Inspector of Ancient Monuments in Wales and Monmouthshire, and from 1936 a notably distinguished Director of the British School at Rome. It would be accurate to describe him then as a rising star in several fields of archaeology. The War that in 1939 curtailed his excavations, a war in which he played a full but sometimes necessarily secret rôle, also prevented the preparation of a full report on his Tintagel results; and irreplaceable material was lost when his Exeter house was bombed in the 1940s. There are, instead, an interim report of 1935, post-war papers on specialized topics, and the successive versions (since 1935) of his official guidebook *Tintagel Castle*.

For almost half a century, Radford's decisive interpretation of the excavated structures and finds proper to Period II, the post-Roman centuries, as those of a Celtic monastery held the field; as did his original conclusion that the Castle – or at any rate the Inner Ward's Great Hall, and the first phase of the Chapel – was built about 1145 by Reginald Earl of Cornwall and then enlarged and completed by Earl Richard in the 1230s. The second contention was linked to the belief that Geoffrey of Monmouth (or, if not him, an eye-witness informant) had seen an actual masonry castle at Tintagel. Since the 1930s, historical and literary research has shown that this is just not possible. Reginald, illegitimate son of King Henry I, was not created earl until 1140, at

least five and possibly more years after any visit by Geoffrey. Though it is not recorded who held the manor of Bossiney (and thus Tintagel) before 1166, it was almost certainly Roger de Mandeville and not the Crown or earldom; the Chapel, if converted (not built) as late as the 1140s, originally had nothing to do with the Castle; there is hardly any twelfth-century pottery from the Island or Castle, almost all of it being thirteenth century (or later); and the Great Hall is an integral part of the 1230s (1233–6) construction by Earl Richard.

Since about 1980, Radford's principal thesis – that the Island was the setting for an Early Christian monastery, beginning in the fifth century – has also had to be abandoned. This happens in archaeology, in Britain and elsewhere, more frequently than may be supposed. It happens in other disciplines, for instance in many of the applied sciences where (as with archaeological research) the pace of discovery for any reason accelerates. Pioneer thinkers learn to accept such disappointments, objectively, as part of the process. But in order to dispel any suggestion of unfair criticism of the excavator, and to understand the background to the 1933 work at Tintagel, we must for a brief while travel back to that period.

Archaeology in Cornwall, where monuments and buildings have been expressed mainly in stone and where past remnants can survive recognizably, has a very long history. Active fieldwork goes back to the early eighteenth century. However, in the 1920s, Cornish antiquarian thinking had lagged badly. It was still perfectly acceptable to give talks to the county's venerable learned societies, founded in George III and IV's reigns, about Druidism, sacred circles, Phoenicians, Danish invaders

41 *Henry Jenner, FSA, first Grand Bard of Cornwall (*photo: Royal Institution of Cornwall*).*

and sun-worship. Londoners, including academic scholars, came to Cornwall for the sea-side, golf or photography; not to interfere unasked. In 1931 the chance discovery of a real, if rather sub-standard, Roman villa at Magor near Camborne led to the formation of a 'Cornwall Excavations Committee'. Chaired by the present writer's grandfather, a County Alderman whose sole archaeological interest lay in establishing the truth of various episodes described in the Old Testament, its prime duty was to raise funds. Enough was found to excavate at Magor and a brash and vigorous young man, Bryan O'Neil, subsequently a wartime Chief Inspector of Ancient Monuments, was invited to supervise the digging. Once formed, the Committee looked around for other sites; it adopted a native Roman-period site (Porth-

meor, Zennor, in the Land's End) where the director, Lt. Colonel Frederick Hirst, broke away to head a new West Cornwall Field Club. In 1936, the Committee wanted to sponsor work at Castle Dore near Fowey, vaguely associated with King Mark, and Mr Ralegh Radford was invited to excavate this small hill-slope fort.

Henry Jenner

Modern, or at any rate contemporary, archaeology had arrived in the deep south-west. Interest was enormous; Porthmeor, to cope with thousands of visitors, had to raise its own corps of lady guides, and local papers printed extended weekly reports. Tintagel had since the nineteenth century always been on the visiting-list for antiquarian outings. Richard Byrn Kinsman, who came from a Falmouth naval and revenue-service family, loved such events, invariably acted as guide (sometimes wearing his special Constable's uniform) and welcomed other savants to join him in impromptu cliff-top lectures. Most such talks were factual, dealing with the visible Castle or the parish church. In 1926 the county's premier learned body, the Royal Institution of Cornwall (founded 1818), included Tintagel in its summer excursion. Kinsman by then was long dead. The on-site lecture, a long one, was given by Mr Henry Jenner, FSA (**41**). Jenner, born 1848 and son of a Rector of St Columb Major, had worked from 1870 to 1909 in the British Museum's Department of Manuscripts and then in the Library, before retiring to Hayle. By 1926, he had been president and editor for almost every society in Cornwall, had produced (1904) a large grammar of the Cornish language and had published papers – still essential reading – on every conceivable aspect of Cornwall's past. He was particularly concerned for the preservation of ancient monuments, and their display (for educational ends) to the public, and had tried to launch a scheme anticipating, by decades, the present arrangements for State care.

Henry Jenner's authority and learning were formidable enough and, within his native Cornwall, unquestioned. Constantly, he wrote in the local newspapers, correcting courteously yet finally the errors and guesses committed by those of lesser knowledge. At Tintagel on this occasion, where his subject was 'Tintagel Castle in History and Romance', he first explained the place in the light of the pre-Norman legends of Mark, Tristan and Iseult; then dealt with Geoffrey of Monmouth and the twelfth-century Arthurian connection; and concluded by saying that, Arthur-wise, 'historically and romantically Tintagel Castle is rather a fraud'. The aged William Taylor, who had brought along his best potsherds to present to the Institution for the museum at Truro, can hardly have been pleased. There on the skyline loomed Taylor's own King Arthur's Castle Hotel, its main sales-point being proximity to the best-known Arthurian site in the west.

Jenner, by then 78, was prodigiously well-read and followed work in all the other Celtic lands. After the party had toured the Island, noting the Chapel, he suggested that it '*may have become a religious establishment of Celtic saints or monks at a later period, and the presence of the evidently Celtic chapel of St Ulyet or Julitta and of Christian interments of perhaps the fifth or sixth century, and the fact that it came into the possession of the monks of St Petrock's, Bodmin, seem to indicate something of the sort.*' (Note the key words, emphasized here with italics.) The great man did end by saying 'But all this must needs be pure conjecture'. To most Cornish people and to many who were not, Henry Jenner's little conjectures had about the same force as a first leader in *The Times*. Some of us will remember the late Sir Mortimer Wheeler having a very similar impact upon lay audiences, stupified by his personality.

Radford's excavations and the 'Celtic monastery'

Given this send-off, and given by 1933 Cornwall's new-found readiness to accept the testimony of the spade, it is understandable that when the young Mr Radford was launched upon Tintagel in 1933, with a remit to get the place ready as a Guardianship site open to all and 'to test the basis of the Arthurian traditions' (about which, as an Oxford-trained historian, he was sceptical), he was from the outset lumbered with all the weight of the Henry Jenner monastic model. The man behind the work, Sir Charles Peers – the Chief Inspector of Ancient Monuments and (1929–33) President of the Society of Antiquaries of London – was himself keenly interested in early monasteries. In 1920 to 1925 Peers had been responsible for excavations, seen in

retrospect as both inadequate and misleading, of the seventh-century Yorkshire monastery at the site of Whitby Abbey. The record of this, reconstructed with difficulty by Radford during the Second World War from a partial archive and published in 1943, including the unearthing of various small component buildings of rectangular form, superficially offered a model for seemingly similar foundations at Tintagel; so, too, did structures found during another very terrible excavation, H.J. Lawlor's of 1922–4 at the monastery of St Mochaoi of Nendrum, County Down, in northern Ireland.

In his first interim report to the Society of Antiquaries (March, 1935) Radford described the seasons of 1933 and 1934 and felt able to say that at Tintagel his excavation 'showed that these buildings belonged to a Celtic monastery . . . The Office of Works had decided to uncover and to preserve the whole of the monastic site'. Visitors had begun to arrive in shoals, to see the digging and to view the restorations (**42**). Radford's Official Guide, good value at only sixpence, appeared first in 1935 – the HMSO printing code is for August – and also stated that one would see 'the remains of a Celtic monastic settlement of a type known in Ireland and in Wales'. Jenner's earlier conjecture – which Jenner never pressed – and possibly Peers's own preference played some part in this. Sixty years on, our reaction must be one of sympathy rather than criticism for a system of working that deprived an excavator of that most valuable of all checks upon solitary

42 *A visit to Tintagel; the Royal Institution of Cornwall's summer excursion, June 1936. The photo shows part of Site A, with the recently-reconstructed walls with turf capping (*photo: G. Penrose*).*

speculation and too-rapid conclusions: the presence on site at all times of professional colleagues (today's assistant directors, site supervisors, finds supervisors, recorders etc.) whose constant discussion and analysis of results makes the director think again and again. Radford was given as a work-force only a band of local men, pure diggers, under a foreman; and because of his other official duties it was not possible for him to be on site except at intervals.

The ground-plan of the excavations, which is a representation of what was selected for digging and above-ground consolidation rather than of everything detectable, even then, is now usually known as 'the HMSO plan' or even 'the old HMSO plan'. Blocks of remains were

43 *Plan of Tintagel Castle and Island (the 'old HMSO plan') with lettered sites, etc. from the second (1939) edition of* Tintagel Castle *by C.A.R. Radford, the official guidebook.*

TINTAGEL CASTLE

given consecutive letters (**43**). Site A, round the Chapel and the first area to be tackled, is recognizable as the faint indications of recti-linear foundations shown on Maclean's plan of sixty years before. Findings here were to some extent in support of the 'Celtic monastery' conclusion. Emphasis was laid, as it had to be in the case of any suspected monastery, on the likely presence of an early Christian monastic cemetery or burial-ground, appropriately near the (later) Chapel. Throughout, this was the weakest part of the whole interpretation. The rock-cut tomb or grave pit ('King Arthur's Bed' or 'Hip-Bath'; the 'Hermites Grave' of Carew in 1602) was of course visible. Three other shal-lower graves, claimed to be rock-cut as well, were found spaced out north of the Chapel. They, too, are probably medieval and in any case a monastic community, claimed to have run into double figures and to have been there for some centuries, cannot possibly be matched by so few burials.

As further parts of the Island's top were opened, and the stones so found used to rebuild the walls season by season – with the HMSO plan having added details, up to the 1939 edition of the guidebook – plans and sections of what had been excavated were made, after digging had finished for the year, by the Office of Works architectural draughtsman, J.A. Wright. These, in pencil with all the dimen-sions noted, form the most valuable sector of the whole archive. By the time the Second World War broke out, the picture of the Celtic monastery at Tintagel had hardened into what was virtually a dogma. Earl Richard's Castle had not been overlooked, conservation of its collapsing masonry rather than exploratory digging being the most pressing need. As for the monastic hypothesis, Radford's scholarship and increasing authority as a widely-travelled expert in such a field, that of the early Church, ensured that it would be accepted for decades to come. A 1942 article ('Tintagel in History and Legend') was the first of many to expand and refine the interpretation. Agriculture ('herb gardens or tiny fields') was proposed, with a monastic populace of between twenty and a hundred monks. Not mentioned, possibly because still concealed by an R.B. Kinsman stone-dump, was the upper part of a large granite rotary-quern or hand-mill of known post-Roman type (**44**), implying that grain was ground here, though not necessarily grown. On

44 *Upper stone of a granite rotary-quern with an eccentric socket for the driving staff, a known post-Roman type; found on the Island (the scale is 40 cm)* (photo: author).

the mainland the Great Ditch with its inner rampart bank, the latter overshadowed by the thirteenth-century Lower Ward outer wall, was said to constitute a massive spiritual boun-dary, the *vallum monasterii* to exclude the sinful outer world, 'erected by the monks'. Until what date this monastery had lasted was left an open question, but slightly later its ending was envisaged as well before the Norman Con-quest – perhaps in the eighth or ninth century.

Methods of excavation at this time, when an Office of Works monument was being investi-gated for subsequent presentation, may not be familiar. The workmen, some of whom had apparently been local quarry workers (the last Tintagel quarry, Long Grass, closed in 1937), were under a trained foreman. Their task was to clear sites on the Island, following and expos-ing walling and keeping an eye open for finds; some sites were established initially by cutting long narrow trial trenches to find foundations. There were, as we saw, no qualified or skilled assistants, and in this respect the Tintagel campaign actually lagged behind contemporary digging in Egypt or Greece, long the butt of contemptuous humour from European excava-tors. Radford's visits were the occasions to assess progress, write up the site notebooks, note the extent and general stratigraphy of what had been found, and deal with whatever diagnostic finds the workmen had happened to

45 *Site B from above, looking eastward (Tintagel Haven, on a rough day, beyond). The neatly-maintained reconstruction of the 1930s has perpetuated a 1930s interpretation (*photo: RCHME*).*

save. By modern standards, there was hardly any sort of day-by-day photographic record, and the few surviving photographs do not portray the actual work, sections, or subsequently concealed details. The 1935 report (10 pages, overall 'HMSO' plan, plans of Site A and the Chapel, three fold-out profiles, seven photographs) covers only the work of 1933 and 1934 – site E (below the Garden), F, G and the Tunnel had not yet been touched – and the three low-level views of Site A show structures, not as exposed, but as they had been neatly rebuilt (**45**). It appears, if only from the Finds Register, that neither the Inner Ward nor the landward Upper and Lower Wards were, in a conventional sense, excavated. Clearance of collapsed overburden did yield some pottery.

The Great Ditch

A significant gap in the record concerns the Great Ditch. This is by any standards a massive piece of work, dug out along a zone of natural fault by a labour-force much in advance of any band of world-excluding monks. It is, though much shorter, on the scale of the Maiden Castle defences. Some great peasant levy was set to work here.

The ditch is mentioned in passing in the literature (though not in the 1935 report, or first guidebook), but only as a *vallum monasterii*. Yet Wright's surviving annotated plans include a record of a long section dug, possibly in 1938, right across the ditch and continued up into the inner rampart bank, inside and outside the high wall of the Lower Ward. Under certain conditions of light and grass, it is possible to detect the line of this narrow cutting. According to entries in the finds register, Period II (post-Roman, imported) pottery was found in the lowest filling of the ditch; and in what from Wright's section – which is schematic and not

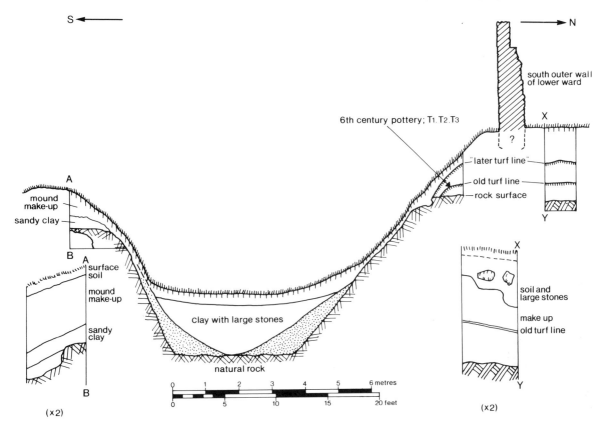

S ←

N →

south outer wall
of lower ward

6th century pottery; T1.T2.T3

X

?

"later turf line"

old turf line

rock surface

Y

A

mound
make-up

sandy clay

B
A

surface
soil

mound
make-up

sandy
clay

B

clay with large stones

natural rock

X

soil and
large stones

make up

old turf line

Y

0   1   2   3   4   5   6 metres

0   5   10   15   20 feet

(×2)   (×2)

46 *Section across the Great Ditch and the inner*
rampart bank below the Lower Ward's outer
wall, drawn by J.A. Wright after the 1938
season; post-Roman pottery from the old land
surface below the rampart included two sherds
of untyped East Mediterranean amphora
(Fabric no.5); three of B.i amphora; two of B.ii
(two different vessels); and eight of B.v (three
different vessels).

marked up as an archaeologist would at the
time – seems to be the Period II old land
surface, under and inside the rampart bank.
Now these are absolutely crucial observations
(**46**). In 1956 Radford returned, still only with a
small gang of workmen, and part-sectioned the
ditch again. This was for the old Ministry of
Works, and unhappily the detailed report sub-
mitted at the conclusion of the work has been
lost. It would now require a *third* sectioning to
confirm this interpretation; but some form of
reconstruction based on Wright's survey and
figures is possible. We have to infer from Geoffrey of Monmouth's description that the three-

men-wide entrance, and therefore the ditch
(and, because it had been dug out, also the
rampart bank), was in existence before the
Castle was built – which implies that it was a
Period II construction; if this is a literary
deduction, the 1930s archaeological evidence
tells the same tale. It is impossible to be certain
that in 1233 the ditch was not cleared out
again, to serve the Castle as its outer line of
defence, but it would be extremely difficult to
show this.

The components of the 'monastery'
Radford's various identifications of his site clusterings (A, B, C etc. – see **43**) on the Island as
components of his monastery are given in the
second edition of the guidebook, which came
out in 1939. Site D, belonging to 'the last period
of the Celtic monastery' – did this mean the
eighth century? – has in the angle of one of its
rooms a feature like a corn-drying oven, or
indeed a medieval baking-oven (**47**), and this
cluster was an agricultural focus. Sites B, C, F
and G with their rectangular foundations were

59

47 *The Island, Site D; corn-drying or baking oven of medieval appearance, originally probably domed (corbelled) with a floor-level flue, in the corner of one of the rooms (photo: author).*

clusters of monastic cells, where the monks lived. Stone benches, primitive heating-flues and other features were pointed out. Sometimes the reconstruction, or the workmen's trenching, failed to find an end-wall (and, looked at in plan now, some of the reconstructions, Site D in particular, seem just plain wrong) and the odd cell was claimed to have been open-ended, the better to provide daylight for those sitting and writing early medieval manuscripts. Of the known water-sources, the one between site B and C was described as 'the monastic well', being covered with a roughly-corbelled vault. The surface of the plateau between site A and the Garden was well and truly trenched, like a gas-main, producing a very long shallow section. It went through what were taken to be low mounds, interpreted as pillow-mounds – that is, artificially-made banks of soil to encourage the burrowing and

breeding of rabbits, used for food. Period II pottery occurred in the trench. What J.A. Wright's section also reveals is that this cutting went across an unrecognized part of a larger complex of structures, linking site A to the foundations exposed much later in the 1984 'Burnt Area' (p. 75). The pillow-mounds are the slight eminences resulting, after a long period of decomposition and slumping, from hut walls made mostly of cut and piled turf on low stone foundations.

Site A, around the Chapel, is complex enough in plan (**48**), and doubly so when an attempt is made to unravel any sequence from it. In 1935, two rectangular rooms – one of a coherent shape, the other scarcely so – were said to be the first buildings on the site, connected with native pottery of third–fourth-century AD type. This led to the suggestion that the Island might have held a small farm, before the monastery was founded. Later buildings or rooms on site A were indicated by the plan, superimpositions and intersections, and the evidence of different styles of walling. The first phase of the Chapel (twelfth century?) concluded the sequence.

A brave attempt was made (1985) by K.R. Dark to present all this in modern terminology.

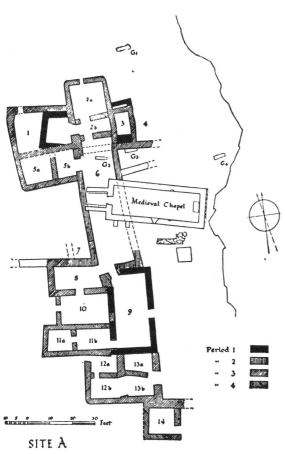

SITE A

48 *Site A. Plan from the second (1939) edition of the official guidebook.* G = *graves, G.4 being 'King Arthur's Bed'. The 'Period 1' structures are those regarded in 1935 as buildings of a Romano-British farm. Room 9 and the main body of the Chapel should be closely compared.*

His reconstruction, summarizing a much longer undergraduate dissertation, relies far too optimistically upon the reported stratigraphy, the various natural and manmade layers; and also introduces the idea that there was one or more phases of building, between the end of Period II activity (around 600? or not long after that?) and the appearance of the Chapel as the start of Period III. This is not, of itself, impossible, though, like Radford before him, Dark failed to appreciate that the top of the Island is probably uninhabitable, or at the least not habitable from choice, during most winters. However, any such episode of occupation between the seventh and eleventh centuries, something for which no other hints can be

found, would be quite devoid of the expected small finds – 'aceramic', or not indicated by datable pottery. Within Cornwall such a state of affairs would be unique because, between 600 and 1100, Cornwall was (unusually) a region where all sorts of pottery continued to be used and made: the imported French class E, grass-marked cooking pots and platters, bar-lug cooking pots with or without grass-marked bases, and by the tenth and eleventh centuries the small Sandy Lane style of pots. Since no examples of any of these have been found on the Island, the immediate conclusion is that the Island was not then inhabited.

The interior of the Chapel was tidied up for display, but not excavated. Nor was it known, until 1988 when the worn turf inside its western porch (or tower-base?) had to be replaced, that immediately below the grass was an undisturbed deposit of Period II occupation rich in post-Roman imported pottery. The making of a full set of phased elevation drawings of the Chapel's walls, and close study of what remains, led Nic Appleton-Fox to conclude – and he was almost certainly right – that the first, Period III (the period around the Norman Conquest), version of the Chapel, had never been a sacred edifice raised from scratch. It was a conversion, its walls built upward upon the existing outline, that happened to be the right shape and approximately east–west, of some long-deserted Period II rectangular cell or room. What this means will be looked at later (p. 111).

The Castle

Radford's reluctance to abandon the idea that construction of at least part of the Castle was due to Earl Reginald in the 1140s had to be combined with the admission that most of it was Earl Richard's. The supposed intersection of the Reginald and Richard periods, with a ninety-year interval, lay in the Inner Ward, where the 1230s Great Hall was claimed to sit on ground retained by, and levelled up within, an outer curtain wall of the 1140s. But the relationship of the two, and the tale of the buttresses (p. 120), rules out any such interval. This does not however mean that there is not, still, ample room for close investigation of the Castle as a medieval complex. On the mainland side the Upper Ward is a peardrop-shaped walled enclosure around the summit of a natural crag, reached by rebuilt stone steps

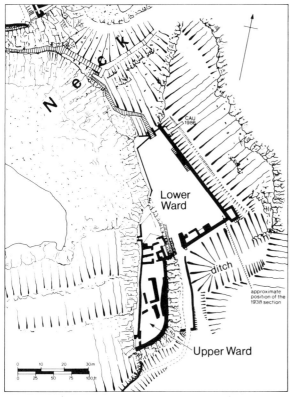

49 *Tintagel Castle; the medieval landward-side Upper and Lower Wards, and the post-Roman Great Ditch (RCHME survey, 1985), showing also the CAU's cutting of 1986 (p. 77) and – dotted line – the approximate position of the 1938 section across the ditch and rampart.*

(**49**). It commands the landward approach, a view across the main way in and down the Great Ditch, the Lower Ward, the nearest part of the Island and a good deal of the coastline in both directions. There would have been the same potential in the post-Roman Period II, when the ditch was made. This raises the interesting thought that, as a natural strongpoint, it may have had some kind of Period II defensive work and if so this could have taken the form of stone walling around the top. Again it is not exactly clear how to show this; but Period II sherds were found within the Upper Ward in the 1930s, and subsequently. They cannot have got there by any *upward* drift from the Lower Ward. Looking at the inside of the existing walling around the southern end (**50**), here and there the basal courses, with large rocks, seem much cruder than the laid medieval course of selected slates above them.

The pottery and its implications for the 'monastery'

In 1956, Radford's descriptive essay on the imported pottery at Tintagel associated with his 'extensive Celtic monastery' and, like it, to be dated 'between the fifth and the eighth or ninth century AD' appeared in the E.T. Leeds memorial volume. It broke new ground, brought together a mass of little-known evidence from other British and Irish sites, and provided a basis for all such further studies. The exotic wheelmade wares at Tintagel were divided into four categories: A, B, C and D. It is now known that class C, jugs or pitchers, are one of many forms of thirteenth-century medieval pottery; class D, with only a few fragments, has been recognized as a grey ware with dark blue-grey-black slip, an Atlantic Gaulish import of the fifth and sixth centuries and a kind of sideline in the main tale. Class A, sub-divided into A.i and A.ii principally because of different fabrics, was a range of finely-made red-slipped bowls and dishes. Class B, far and away the largest of all – today amounting to three or four thousand sherds – covered all the amphorae, the large handled jars to hold liquids (**51**). A 'considerable number of varieties of forms and wares, suggesting several sources' was mentioned but no sub-division, as with class A, was then attempted.

In a series of papers, 1954 to 1959, the present writer took up study of these imported wares because more and more excavated sites in Cornwall and Scilly, let alone elsewhere in the British Isles, were starting to yield examples. It was possible first to show that the fine dishes A.i and A.ii were, respectively, the known Late Roman C and Late Roman B wares of Mediterranean archaeology – LRB (for short) coming from North Africa, probably Tunisia and Carthage, and LRC from somewhere in Asia Minor. Secondly, there were also clear divisions within Class B: four, B.i to B.iv, were described, their Insular (i.e. British plus Irish) distributions set out, and even at that early stage parallels from the eastern half of the Mediterranean could be shown from the literature and from museums.

Since then, following Dr John Hayes's work, the actual names of 'African Red Slip Ware' and 'Phocaean Red Slip Ware' have been substituted for the former A.ii/LRB and A.i/LRC, but the notational system of B.i, B.ii etc., passed into general use and was even trans-

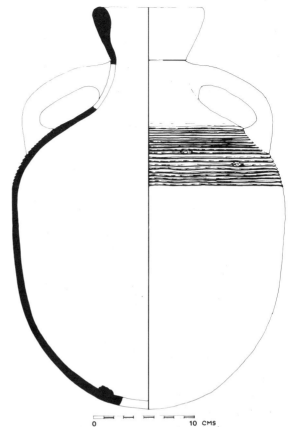

50 *Inside the Upper Ward, the curved southern end; are the lowest five or six courses, below the eroded mortared medieval stonework, possibly post-Roman?* (photo: author).

51 *A Class B.i amphora, of eastern Mediterranean origin, from Tintagel. The section profile (*left*) shows how thin-walled such vessels can be. The band of 'combed' ornamentation is a continuous spiral groove, made by impressing a point into the wet clay and slowly moving it upwards as the pot turns on the wheel.*

ferred back from British to Mediterranean site reports. In 1988, as the proper cataloguing of thousands of Tintagel finds took place, it could be shown that while the well-defined B.i, B.ii and B.iv, with a new group called B.v, still held good, the one-time B.iii – 'Miscellaneous' – had dissolved into a long run of untyped amphorae, some represented by only a few sherds, and even some coarse wares that were cooking vessels rather than containers. What this may mean is examined later (p. 133).

Radford's work on this pottery, a contribution to knowledge whose importance in 1956 cannot be too highly appreciated, confirmed (in outline) the Continental and Mediterranean sources, and the probable date-range from the fifth to early seventh centuries AD. He provided some clues from the few literary sources about such long-distance contact, with its interpretation as trade; the goods sought in Cornwall

were likely to have included tin – streamed tin in ingot form. He went no further because the Island was still being presented as a monastery; post-Roman contact with mainland Europe was to be seen in terms of the spreading of Christian influence, and the amphorae from the East were, it was implied, mostly to hold wine for the Communion. The impressive nature and location of Tintagel as an early, indeed *the* early Celtic monastic establishment, with the authority of the excavator and of his pronouncements, coloured most thinking about these imports for the next 25 years. As more and more excavated places produced pieces of Class A or Class B pottery, or both together,

63

the distribution maps were constantly having to be updated. Some larger sites inland, like the reused hillfort of South Cadbury Castle on the Somerset–Wiltshire border, identified as the Arthurian 'Camelot' and dug in the 1960s with much panache and publicity, yielded a hundred or more sherds.

While all such items brought from afar in boats must, as a matter of course, have been first unloaded somewhere on early Britain's Atlantic shores, no proper distinction was being made between such primary importation-points and any secondary recoveries from places the vessels had been carried to well inland. Nor did it seem to be grasped that entirely different interpretations were necessary for the thousands of fragments, from a hundred vessels at least, at Tintagel, and for the two or three sherds from Cornish sites like the hillslope fort of Killibury a few miles inland. In the setting of fifth–sixth-century Cornwall and Scilly, where possibly only four out of some thirty places at which this imported pottery has been found can now figure as (coastal) points of immediate importation or unloading, the challenge became that of explaining – in the face of what Radford had written – just *how* an isolated clifftop community of holy men, monks living in stark poverty, could come to dominate an entrepreneurial network.

To claim with hindsight that most of the clues existed may not seem tremendously helpful, but it is a claim that would be justified. In Chapter 6, the present and fresh explanations make up a model that, in 1960, would not actually have been feasible; at that date, several necessary lines of research had not yet begun. The intervention of methods drawn from geology and mineralogy, making the analysis of pottery fabrics a commonplace device, so linking sherd and source through means other than simply visual similarity, was a considerable step forward. So too, from economic history, was a special concern with amphorae as indicators of trade in the Old World. While for most of us it is always exciting to see and to handle quantities of unfamiliar potsherds dug up at remote locations – or to crunch along a deserted beach on the island of Crete, consisting not of little pebbles and sea-shells but mainly of amphora fragments, B.i and B.ii among them – all this amounts to nothing more than the discarded Coca-Cola cans and beer bottles of the early first millennium AD. As

Radford wrote, 'No one will suppose that the large coarse vessels were imported for their own sake and not for their contents'. The trouble has been that, on occasions, hard-working excavators toiling at remote sites with virtually no small finds, and finally recovering a few pieces of B.ii amphora, have understandably forgotten to ask the right questions.

It is difficult to know what to write, fairly, above the 1930s Office of Works excavations at Tintagel. It may, even in 1992, be too early to do so; the present investigations in their turn could well be discredited at some future date. Radford's was by no means the sole campaign whose initial premiss, put forward well before the digging had started, limited the excavator's choices; nor the only one where in later years a radical rethinking became necessary. A long 1990s critique of the methodology of the 1930s would be as unjust in this case as it would be in brain surgery or the use of radio telescopes. The bonus was that the essential *evidence* was produced, and largely seen for what it was.

The churchyard in wartime

A second, though very much smaller, investigation must be described to round off this chapter. Edward Arundell FSA, Vicar of Tintagel from 1938 to 1945, had antiquarian tastes. In 1940, aided by the builder George Climo, he dug below the south chancel wall inside Tintagel church – examining a so-called Founder's Tomb – and they broke into a crypt with several coffins. Fragmentary notes, since lost, described this. During 1942 Mr Arundell moved outside; north-west of the tower was a stump of granite sticking out of the grass, taken to be either part of a cross-base or all that was left of the shaft of a cross. At the time, there was at Treligga a few miles south a firing range manned by Navy and RAF personnel and Arundell persuaded some off-duty airmen to help him. As far as can now be established, the vicar and the Boys in Blue began by digging out the stump, which turned out not to be a cross-shaft at all, but a partly-shaped pillar of granite nearly 2 m (6½ ft) high. There is, and was then, in the northern part of the churchyard a group of mysterious grass-covered mounds (**52**) and the granite pillar had stood close to the largest, Mound C. The party probably began, armed with picks and shovels, by attacking a corner of Mound D, which has certainly been dug into, and almost as certainly

52 *Tintagel churchyard; Mound D from the south, 1989 (the pole is scaled in bands of 0.5m) (photo: RCHME).*

consisted in its upper layer of builder's rubble and discarded roof-slates. They then moved to Mound C, along whose east–west (longer) axis they sunk a deep irregular trench, the spill being thrown out to the east. About 1.5 to 2 m (5 to 6½ ft) below the mound's grassy summit, they came across two slate-lined graves, and also laid open the end of a more elaborate grave indicated by a low wall of horizontally-laid slates (**53**). Some bones were found, with 'glazed' (i.e. medieval or later) pottery. The end of the venture is not known, except for the fact – established in 1990 – that the Mound C trench was not filled in. Perhaps the airmen became bored, and failed to report again.

A few old people in and around Tintagel still vaguely recall Vicar Arundell doing something in the churchyard. Most of the folk closely associated with the church were away on active service, or have since died, and would-be oral historians might like to note that, for this fifty-year interval, it has proved impossible to find anyone who can remember any of the details. Arundell's notes were seen by A.C. Canner, who makes passing reference to them in his *The Parish of Tintagel*, but they are now lost (and cannot have been all that specific).

Fortunately, a real archaeologist – the late C.K. Croft Andrew FSA – was then excavating in the district, engaged by the Ministry of Works on prehistoric barrows threatened by airfield construction around Bodmin Moor. Mr

Croft Andrew visited the churchyard when Arundell's digging was more or less finished. He took four black-and-white snaps, and these with the negatives were placed in a labelled and dated envelope which passed through various hands, unopened and unexamined, until in 1984 it ended up at the Cornwall Archaeological Unit. New, enlarged, prints caused considerable excitement.

For Croft Andrew's visit, the granite pillar or menhir was propped upright with bits of wood (**54**). Since it weighs a quarter of ton – it was neatly re-erected in 1990 – some of the airmen must have been around to lift it. Two photographs show the menhir. The other two, taken from the east looking along the Mound C trench (and Croft Andrew marked compass-points on a print), have enough detail to show that the body of the mound was artificial, with layers; that the cist graves, east–west Christian burials, lie about 2 m (6½ ft) down; and that the end of the more elaborate grave protrudes from the uneven south face of the trench.

This 1942 'excavation', which if now repeated in the same manner would be not only improper but, under ecclesiastical law, grossly irregular – there is no evidence that Arundell had official permission – was sufficient, with the existing surveys, to allow a model sequence for the history of the churchyard to be written (1988). The new hypothesis, of a sequence spanning perhaps fifteen centuries, was interesting enough to frame detailed proposals when in 1989 the offer of sponsorship by Mobil North Sea Limited made the idea of controlled excavation at last possible. This time, full con-

65

54 *Tintagel churchyard: the granite pillar, dug out in 1942, propped up for the occasion. It was then left lying on the grass and re-erected in 1990 (photo: C.K. Croft Andrew).*

53 *A view from east to west along Mr Arundell's trench through Mound C, 1942, showing (*left*) the end of a slate-built grave and (*bottom, centre*) the side-slab of a long cist (*photo: C.K. Croft Andrew).*

sultation with the present Vicar, Ivan Gregory SSC, the parochial church council and the parishioners, and the grant of a Diocesan faculty, placed the work on the correct footing and allowed a start in the spring of 1990. What happened then, and in 1991, is related in Chapters 6 and 7. Because of Croft Andrew's timely arrival, we can perhaps forgive Arundell's enthusiasm. The revelation of what lay deep down below Mound C was the most important point.

5

Deconstruction of

a monastery

During the 1970s, in respect of Tintagel and its ancient and increasingly visited monuments two quite separate lines of archaeological research were (unknown to the general public) slowly converging. One concerned the finds, mostly pottery, nearly all housed at Truro. The other concerned the continued presentation of the Island as the site of an Early Christian monastery. By 1970 television treatment had nudged archaeology into a rating somewhat higher than angling, though a long way below football, and people who were becoming familiar with terms like 'the Dark Ages' naturally wanted to know more when they walked around supposed Dark Age remains.

Radford at Tintagel in the 1930s was, not for the only time, something of an archaeological pioneer. Plenty of large Anglo-Saxon sites had been explored in the eastern half of England; relatively few of the same general date in the western, or Atlantic, half. In 1935 virtually nothing was known about post-Roman Cornwall when it came to the matter of dirt archaeology and small finds. There was a small group of early but undated foundations of little stone-walled churches – some with signboards claiming 'Founded in AD 500' – and a larger group of, also undated, granite crosses. It was still not clear whether the Cornish, between Roman and Norman times, had really made and used domestic pottery, engaged in agriculture, or lived in stone cabins instead of circular thatched huts. Nor were such questions ever seriously posed. County histories stated that there had been local kings with names like Gereint and Constantine, and monasteries as well as little churches. But again nobody, not even Henry Jenner with his considerable archaeological interests, seems to have asked

what a kingly stronghold or a pre-Norman monastery actually looked like. And any kind of systematic digging to find answers to those puzzles began, as we saw earlier (p. 54), only with the Cornwall Excavations Committee in 1931.

Deciphering the pottery

Radford's recognition that the unexpectedly large amounts of non-local, reddish, wheelmade pottery found at Tintagel had all been imported from Spain or Gaul or the lands around the eastern Mediterranean opened a new chapter. By 1980, more finds of such pottery from Britain and Ireland were being regularly reported. In 1983, when the Museum of the Royal Institution of Cornwall at Truro planned a new and enlarged display of Tintagel material, the writer was asked to take a fresh look at what was available. This led to a happy period of pure detective-work, the kind of activity that archaeologists often dream about: a chance to get to grips with primary material not seen for years. Under an agreement made with the Duchy of Cornwall in the 1940s, all the Tintagel finds – except for a small batch of pottery from the Island's Sites A and C, deposited for reference at the British Museum in 1949 – were to be housed at Truro. Regardless of whatever agency administers Tintagel, the finds of course remain the property of the Duchy. It took a little while to bring the material together; a larger batch had at some stage been lent, not given, to the British Museum (and forgotten about), eight boxes of unmarked and unwashed sherds were lurking in a Department of the Environment store boxed up as 'Roman amphorae' and 'medieval ridge-tiles' (though in fact neither), and a small

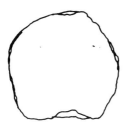
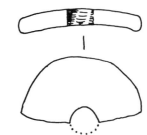
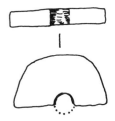

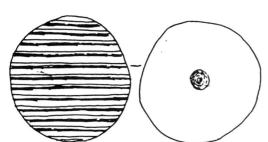
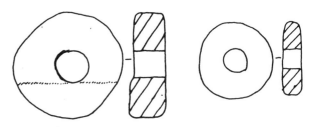

55 *Spindle-whorls made from imported pottery.* (Top row*) Tintagel, incomplete disc and two broken whorls, all African Red Slip ware.* (Bottom row*) From Gwithian, west Cornwall, all from B.i amphora fragments.* (*Scale bar 5 cm.*)

but choice collection, in the 1950s wired to boards as a display in what was then a combined ticket-office and tea-house at Tintagel, was being privately stored.

Once the entire collection had been re-assembled, unpacked, if necessary carefully washed (much of it was still as the workmen in the 1930s had put it into paper sacks) and laid out for examination, important new facts became apparent. The supposed 'Roman amphora' and 'ridge-tile' fragments, some the size of a modern saucer, were from six or more huge vessels 1 m (3¼ ft) high, labelled as Class B.v for want of a more precise term, and very similar to a known North African variety used in the fourth to seventh centuries for the carriage of olive oil, but in fact now thought, from the composition of the clay, to be an unlocated East Mediterranean type. An early aim was to work out minimum totals of the different kinds of amphorae represented. This task involves, not trying to stick together and thus entirely to reconstruct the original pots, but counting; the system is easy enough. Taking, for instance, a class of amphora like B.i, which possesses a

very distinctive fabric and of which all known examples anywhere always have two handles, then the existence of three handles *must* imply a minimum of two such vessels; if out of seventeen handles, say, ten prove to be five matched pairs and the remaining seven are all individual, the minimum total will be twelve; if there are pieces of three rim-circuits, all B.i but of slightly different profiles, and no handles at all, the minimum would be three. (Counts are preferably based on handles, of which there are plenty from Tintagel.)

The totals began to climb up into double figures, and other facts emerged. All these pots, which must have been originally imported for what they contained, had at some stage been broken; some sherds had then been chipped to a rough circle, ground into a regular circle, and pierced to form spindle-whorls (little fly-wheels of pottery), for a wooden spindle on which a yarn is spun up (**55**). This habit has been recorded, using similar sherds of imported wares, on other sites in Devon and Cornwall. However, there were also larger and cruder chipped discs which, as in the Mediterranean, had been brought to Tintagel in that form because they could be recognized as amphora-stoppers, pieces fixed with pitch or some such substance into the narrow neck of a vessel to seal its liquid content (**56**). Again, it was a very common custom in the Eastern Mediterranean and in Egypt, when a whole batch of amphorae

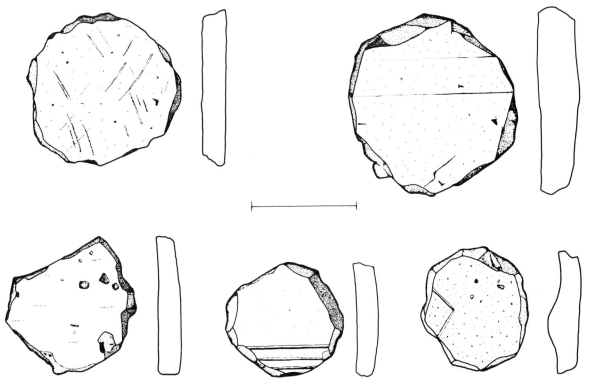

56 *Tintagel: chipped, roughly circular discs of pottery (both typed and untyped amphorae), used with some fixative as 'neck-stoppers' for filled amphorae in cargo. (Drawn by Carl Thorpe; scale bar 5 cm.)*

containing wine or oil was ready, to mark the vessels on the shoulder or neck in a red or black pigment with batch or lading marks (*dipinti*, 'painted' marks) indicating source, shipper, contents and capacity (**57**). In these eastern provinces of the Late Roman Empire, where nearly all the Tintagel amphorae were produced, Greek was the common language, and the dipinti are thus in Greek letters, or used Greek letters for abbreviations or as numerals. A very few Tintagel sherds, mostly B.ii, still bore the faintest traces of red dipinti. But one or two other pieces from the shoulders of the same kinds of amphorae had other markings, scratched on them at a secondary stage (*graffiti*, 'scratched' marks). These included most of one with XIV, the Roman numeral *quatuordecim* – 14 (**58**). It was then realized that in a collection of similar pottery found at Mothecombe in South Devon there were sherds with what was described as 'lattice marks' that seemed to be the remains of XXV – 25. Mark-

ings of this sort imply the *western* provinces of the Empire, where Latin was the commercial tongue of the wharves and the warehouses. Does this suggest a stage of trans-shipment, between the East and Tintagel? And, as the process of identification continued, how could the arrival of a trading-ship from the East be explained, whose cargo consisted, not of several hundred amphorae of the same kind, but several hundred amphorae of five or six different kinds? Finally, how also could the presence, along with amphorae and the red slip-ware plates (attractive space-fillers and cargo embellishments), be accounted for, of things like pans and skillets – as they seem to be – which if carried on a ship of the sixth century would be not cargo but the conventional fittings of the galley?

There were problems in the 1983 sort-out of another kind. While there was no doubt that all the finds came from the Island (with a few from the mainland side), only some 10 per cent had ever been marked with locations – 'Site B', 'N. of Chapel', 'Garden' and so forth. When several hundred pieces of locally-made (and superficially third–fourth-century AD native Roman period) pottery had been put aside, and also a much larger quantity of obviously medieval,

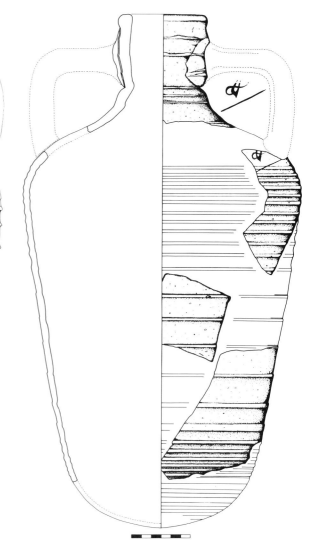

57 *Examples of Class B.ii amphorae, most widely travelled of the eastern Mediterranean fifth – sixth-century exports (from the Cilician coastal belt). (*Left*) From Tintagel; (*right*) from a small unexcavated monastic site in the Tell-el-Amarna crescent, Egypt (note traces of red dipinti on the shoulder). (Drawn by Carl Thorpe.)*

mostly thirteenth-century pottery, the main bulk – the Period II imports – was insufficiently provenanced. The slow task of going through all the unmarked pieces and then matching them with, or even joining them to, the marked pieces had to be attempted. Gradually it became clear that the main focus of the imported material, all the bits of broken amphorae and the smashed red-ware dishes

(and also a few tiny scraps of contemporary glass, probably of Egyptian manufacture), was centred on the Inner Ward, spreading out to Site A round the Chapel and also Site B (**59**). Beyond this over the top of the Island, finds tailed off, so that almost nothing had been discovered at Site D. This is all very well, but the main feature of the Inner Ward is of course the Great Hall and ancillary rooms of the thirteenth century, which does not explain why this spot should have been important seven centuries earlier.

In 1988, sponsored by English Heritage, all the finds were at last properly catalogued; and this included a good many, post-1930s, surface finds from various spots on the Island. At least three implications became apparent. First of

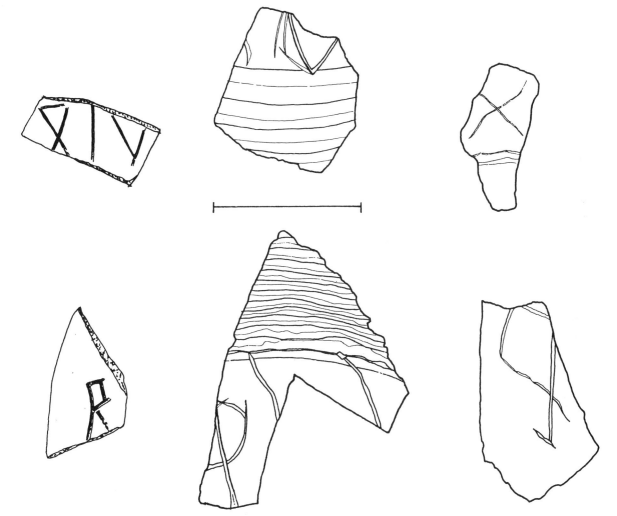

58 *Graffiti on amphora sherds, mostly B.i, from Tintagel. (*Top row*) A clear 'XIV' (14) and possibly part of 'XV' (15). The uncertain 'X' may be the Greek letter* chi *(= 600); (*lower row*) the Greek letter* rho *(R), used to denote 100. (Scale bar, 5 cm.)*

all, the quantity of imported pottery from Tintagel could be shown to be not only dramatically greater than that from any other single site dated to about AD 450–600 in either Britain or Ireland, but also larger than the combined total of *all* such pottery from *all* known sites; and, given that only about 5 per cent of the Island's accessible surface has been excavated or examined, the original total of imports may well have been on the scale of one or more complete shiploads – with individual ships perhaps carrying a cargo of six or seven hundred amphorae. Secondly, taking the simplest view that the least unlikely explanation for the presence of such goods would be an aspect of trade, would this really be consistent with the idea of an ascetic Christian monastery in a remote coastal setting? If trade, what was being traded, and if trade-goods had to be bought in, what wealth was being used to buy them? Furthermore, how can (on the one hand) a Great Ditch be interpreted as a *vallum monasterii*, a barrier to exclude the outer world from a community of prayer and solitude, and (on the other) this evidence of wholly worldly activity within the same barrier be explained? Thirdly (and this is not to be pounced upon as a sexist observation), spindle-whorls imply the preparation of yarn, probably from plucked wool of sheep, which was a fairly specialized craft carried out by women. Was this then not a

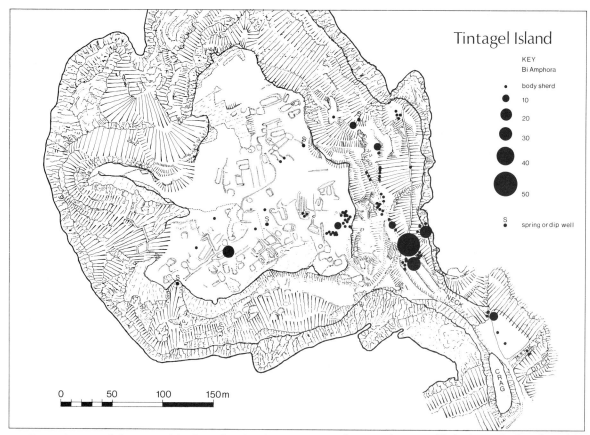

Tintagel Island

KEY
Bi Amphora

·   body sherd

●   10

●   20

●   30

●   40

●   50

S   spring or dip well

0   50   100   150m

59 *Distributional density of finds – sherds of the main types of imported pottery. A bias toward the excavated areas is balanced by such factors as uneven recovery from the surfaces of paths, the relatively small quantity from the Burnt Area and a total absence from Site D and the Tunnel.*

monastery in the accepted sense? It is not clear that early monks in Atlantic Britain spun their own yarn.

The other line of research was, on the whole, independent of re-examination of the finds. It arose more from a re-examination of the nature of the excavated structures, their character and their plan. In the 1930s, remnants of medieval mansions were known alongside the whole range of castles and churches large or small, but the contemporary peasant homestead formed a topic as obscure as it was also thought unimportant. In 1965, this had changed. Excavation since the Second World War had begun to bring to light instances, some in south-west Britain, of the humble houses used by farmers, pastoralists and tin-streamers between the eleventh and fourteenth centuries, in some cases with pottery and other small finds to match. Visitors to Tintagel Island, not the happy summertime visitors in search of Arthurian scenery, but archaeologists who knew more and more about the landscape of the Middle Ages, were beginning to ask awkward questions. Some of them commented that the rectangular remains, the reconstructed wallings of the supposed monastic cells on Sites B and D, bore a noticeable resemblance to peasant buildings of post-Norman date. Site D in particular came in for a good deal of informed criticism, as it was presented (**60**). Its reconstruction is certainly odd. The long narrow space between the 'cells', a space left open as if it had been a kind of passage open to the sky, has a central stone fireplace or hearth. This becomes less odd, when it is realized that the space is probably the main structure and the other elements are side-rooms, and that missing end-walls from the main structure must have been used to

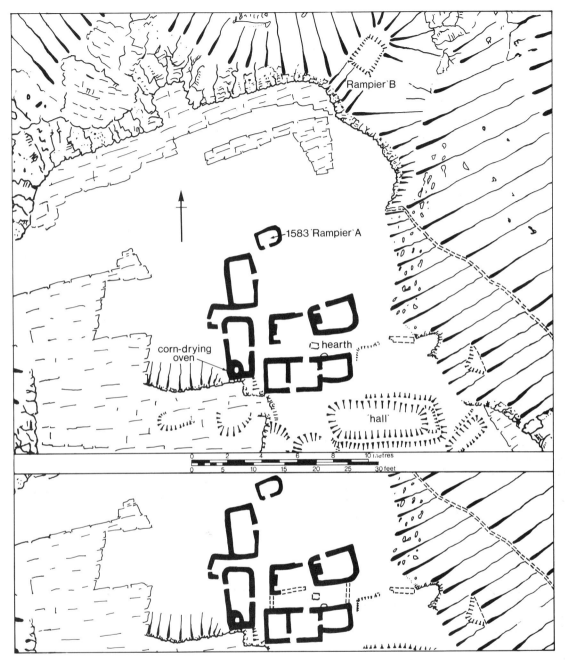

60 *The Island, Site D, from the RCHME survey.* (Above) *As reconstructed, showing also positions of the 1583 'Rampiers A and B' and the elongated foundations of the 'Hall' (p. 91).* (Below) *A possible alternative reconstruction.*

build the 1583 rampier recommended by Grenville (p. 50). The corbelled oven in one of the Site D rooms, it was noticed, looks completely medieval. Is this because the oven, and indeed the whole site, *is* medieval?

Again, if in the 1930s there were hardly any detailed plans of large-scale monasteries from post-Roman western Britain, in the 1960s and 1970s a very fair if generalized picture had

been built up from excavations, aerial photography and field surveys. Where, on the Island, were all the expected and normally

73

encountered features of a typical monastery? The Chapel could not be shown on Radford's evidence to be any older than the twelfth (or just possibly late eleventh) century; certainly not to be of the sixth or seventh century. There was no monastic cemetery, the few graves being insufficient for this and probably of medieval date. No other monastery in the remote West, older than the arrival of the English, was known to have these clusters of large rectangular cells where the brethren lived and worked.

A proper archaeological link between the remains of these cells and the Period II imported pottery had neither been demonstrated nor published and given the standard of excavation practised in the 1930s, with its defective records, in all probability never could be. Among the thousands of small finds, nothing, no single item, unquestionably and exclusively Christian or monastic had ever been brought to light. Lastly, aside from whatever closing date could be attached to the imported pottery as the main index of date on the site (agreed to be about 600–650), the point at which this monastery came to an end had never been clearly stated, and Radford's own estimates had fluctuated, with a slight preference for perhaps around AD 800. This raised a different problem. It was not wholly impossible, but it was becoming more and more improbable as an idea, that so large, so prominent and above all so materially rich a monastery could have vanished or left no trace, historically speaking. There were other early monasteries in Cornwall, unexcavated, but as far as is known all reflected in historical sources.

The Scottish Archaeological Forum

At an archaeological symposium held in Scotland in 1973, one within the annual Scottish Archaeological Forum series, the chosen theme was 'Early Celtic Monasteries'. Dr Ian Burrow read a short paper with the title of 'Tintagel – Some Problems'. He voiced most of the objections just described, and added a few more, commonly held by then among most specialist students of post-Roman Britain. The suggested outcome was that Radford's model of there having been an early Christian monastery at Tintagel was no longer one that could be sustained, and certainly not on the evidence that was available in print. It is much harder to deconstruct the conclusions of some past campaign that has never been published in full

than it would be to reinterpret, from a mass of printed detail, a long and long-accepted report. Nor was the occasion rendered less uncomfortable for the speaker by the fact that the excavator was sitting in the audience, preparing to sum up the proceedings at the end.

Ian Burrow's preferred new model ('a quite drastic reappraisal') abandoned the idea of any monastery, probably for good as far as the professional audience was concerned. He had in mind, instead, a defended secular stronghold, one in which the visible and rebuilt cells, or the clusters like Site B, were not as early as Period II at all. 'There is a strong possibility that they are of wholly later date, in which case the structures associated with the fifth- to seventh-century material still await discovery.' The abundant pottery, he hinted, might then have to be explained in terms of a trading-post, or even a market; a commercial centre maintained at 'a settlement with a differing social status from that implied by the term *stronghold*'. Burrow, and others who had been concerned with looking at many post-Roman fortified sites large and small in western and northern Britain, closed by suggesting that the most likely model for the Island, defended as it was on the land side by a great ditch and bank that Radford himself claimed was constructed in Period II, would be a royal citadel or centre – and that the presence of exotic imported goods should be assessed in that light.

If the intellectual dissolution of this particular monastery can be dated from Burrow's lecture, and its publication in 1974, the excavator did not relinquish his own interpretation. In 1975 when the International Arthurian Society, concerned in the main with the 'Arthur' of European medieval literature and legend, held an August conference at Exeter, Radford was co-author of a handsome booklet describing Arthurian sites in south-west Britain. His chapter on Tintagel made little or no concession to revisionism. Indeed, it re-stated the belief – by 1975, quite untenable – that an original (if smaller) Castle had been built by Earl Reginald at the earliest possible year he could have done so as the earl (1141), and that Geoffrey of Monmouth 'wrote his *Historia* at the time when the first castle on the island was under construction'. A new, but unconvincing, artistic reconstruction of the Site B cluster was shown. The abandonment of the monastery was left chronologically open ('nothing on the site suggests a date later than the eighth century').

The Burnt Area

In the extremely dry late summer of 1983, a fire was somehow started on the Island, by the south-west part of its top. Here the soil above slate bedrock was less than a foot deep, matted with roots. Smouldering unchecked for some weeks, the fire spread along underground, affecting about one-third of the whole plateau and also causing minor burning on the lower South Terrace. After some time, it was doused by local firemen, who had to pump up sea-water; the salt prevented any natural regeneration of the turf.

When the 1984 visitor season reopened at Easter, the site custodians reported that people were wandering unchecked over the burnt area, kicking up ash and stones. The former soil cover had been reduced to a pinkish-grey ashy layer, quantities of which were being blown away in gales or washed off by heavy rain. Eventually, in late 1985 with CAU staff on hand to monitor the result of any disturbance to the site, the area was re-seeded, with forced pumping of fresh water – a Royal Navy helicopter was needed to lift in the heavy plant for this – to which nutrients and selected grass-seed had been added. Three years later, the fence could be removed and the vegetation cover seems to have become established, on a thinner soil-base.

The 1985 survey

When Ian Burrow had hinted that any post-Roman, Period II structures might have looked quite different from the visible, 1930s-reconstructed, cells, and could even have been 'as yet unrecognized slight timber structures on the site', he had not known of J.A. Wright's season-by-season plans and sections of the excavated areas. These, with what can be seen still as short lengths of seemingly lower walling visible underneath the larger and mainly rectangular cells, pointed to the possibility of Period II huts, or rooms, or buildings, probably smaller in size than anything reconstructed for display and also probably with some kind of stone footings to their walls.

Clearly the question of which huts, or cells, or whatever the rectangular buildings are called, belong to which period of the past has from the start lain at the core of any interpret-

ation. This is why in the decades after the Second World War the suspicion that the reason Radford's many monastic 'cells' looked like medieval buildings was because they *were*, in fact, medieval buildings, became a majority viewpoint; even if it was not expressed in print. It left unsolved of course the riddle of what structures (if any) had accompanied the Period II finds.

Not long before the episode of the fire, the writer and Dr Peter Fowler – then Secretary of the Royal Commission on the Historical Monuments of England (RCHME) – spent some time examining the Island in detail. We had concluded, from surface indications, that all the reconstructed clusters like Site A, B, F and so on were never isolated aspects of any dispersed occupation, monastic or not, but simply those parts most easily spotted in 1933 and singled out for excavation. They stood out, artificially, from a complex of land-use covering most of the 4.5 ha (11 acres) of the Island's top. We noticed many other remains, some of them strings of more or less continuous walled constructions below the tussocky turf, on the slope below Site A and the Chapel, and on the lower South Terrace. What most of these suggested to us was nothing to do with Period II, but the remnants of activity belonging to Period IV, the time of the Castle's existence. An explanation was another matter. An 'island town' was ruled out by the factors discussed already (Chapter 3). What would its inhabitants have done? Why would they want to live here? How would they have maintained a water-supply, combined livestock with plots in so crowded a space, enjoyed a normal medieval economy? Our eventual suggestion (and for the moment it has to stand, simply because nothing less unconvincing has been put forward) is that most of the rectangular huts were the thirteenth-century version of the contractor's Portakabins one sees clustered at the start of twentieth-century motorways. They were quarters, built for the labour force engaged on Earl Richard's Castle, and perhaps used off and on for not more than a few years.

During 1984 and 1985, frequent visits to the burnt area by CAU staff confirmed, disquietingly, what the custodians were reporting. In tramping around the ashy debris, visitors – as well as wind and rain – were uncovering burnt, but recognisable, sherds of pottery, and the last remnants of what seemed to be foundations of

61 *The surface of the Burnt Area on the Island, June 1984; a typical short and slightly curving row of large slates – the foundation-course for a turf-walled hut* (photo: author).

small buildings (**61**). Though converted by fire to the same dark-grey colour, the potsherds were (to the expert eye) without exception pieces of amphorae of known types. None of them was medieval. Nor were there traces of the higher walling of the larger rectangular huts. Was this, then, an exposed surface belonging to Period II only?

RCHME was therefore invited in 1985 to produce a new and total, 1:500 scale analytical survey of the whole of the Island, to record the traces now being reported from occasional fieldwork and to include the precious remnants exposed by the fire, since the Burnt Area would have to be prepared, given a shallow raking, re-seeded and closed off before another winter devastated it. The three Royal Commissions (England, Scotland, Wales) operate in the field to the highest standard of accuracy and presentation, large-scale set piece surveys of this kind being constantly in demand. The work was carried out by Messrs Norman Quinnell FSA and Martin Fletcher, who most fortunately already knew the place intimately because, when with the field staff of the Ordnance Survey's Archaeology Division (now disbanded), they had undertaken map revision there (**colour plate** 4).

The resulting plan, which corrected errors in the old HMSO plan, provided new fixed points

and at last gave a proper basis for all future work, was rapidly published at reduced scale with a commentary by RCHME. On its own it could not solve all the archaeological riddles. The confirmation that the top of the Island was, to all intents, one vast and continuous site with a hundred or more components, something far more intricate than had ever been demonstrated, aroused wide interest. Immediately, it was clear that there were at least two kinds of building-foundations (the larger, rectilinear, supposedly medieval ones; much smaller and less substantial ones, as in the Burnt Area) and several sorts of groupings or clusterings. Immediately, too, those concerned with monastic archaeology could see that no Celtic monastery so far identified elsewhere looked anything like this.

In 1985, then, precisely fifty years after Radford had first expounded the nature of his Celtic monastery to the Society of Antiquaries, two (or more) lines of research and reassessment had come together: the extraordinary corpus of portable finds had been placed in its national, and even wider, context demanding a new and appropriate explanation; and the revelation of the full physical nature of the site confirmed earlier pressure that fresh models were needed. The monastic establishment had at last been deconstructed, and the choice of this particular term to mark its dissolution becomes appropriate when it is remembered (p. 55) how that particular model first arose. Since then, a number of minor investigations have taken place. Some arose because various works under the heads of maintenance or repair were executed on the Island without the desirable archaeological supervision, exposing features that demanded subsequent archaeological attention. All are relevant to the interpretation, period by period, offered in the following two chapters.

1986: Lower Ward

Early in 1986, during the kind of weather requiring a visitor to cling to the wet grass to avoid being blown over the edge, Cornwall Archaeological Unit was commissioned by English Heritage to investigate parts of the (mainland) Lower Ward, in advance of some engineering work – an improved drainage system and the insertion of rock anchors to stabilize the seaward end of the medieval walling.

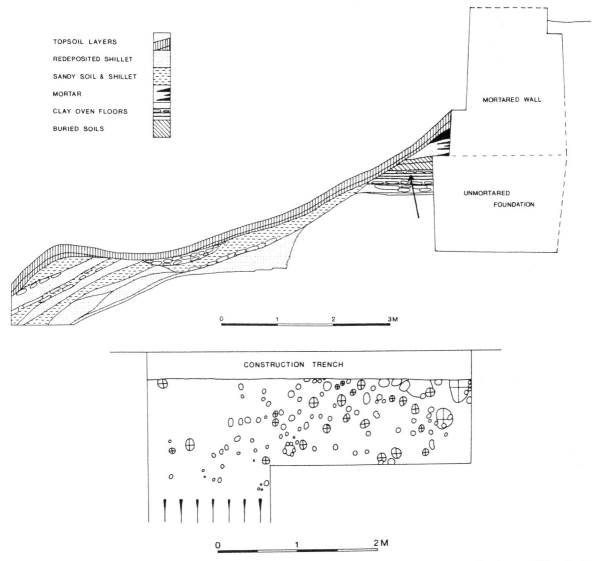

TOPSOIL LAYERS
REDEPOSITED SHILLET
SANDY SOIL & SHILLET
MORTAR
CLAY OVEN FLOORS
BURIED SOILS

MORTARED WALL

UNMORTARED FOUNDATION

0   1   2   3M

CONSTRUCTION TRENCH

0   1   2 M

62 *Post-Roman occupation found in the CAU's 1986 cutting outside the north-east corner of the Lower Ward. (Above) The section (south side) against the remains of the thirteenth-century Lower Ward wall; the central clay-oven floor or hearth (arrowed) gave an archaeomagnetic date of AD 450–500. (Below) Plan (of the area against the wall) of stake- or post-holes, those more than 10 cm (4 in) deep being crossed. (Drawn by Stephen Hartgroves.)*

It had already been suspected, because of casual finds of imported pottery there in the 1930s and because, too, the rampart within the Great Ditch enclosed this area of the landward part of the citadel, that post-Roman, Period II occupation might underlie the Lower Ward. A fairly large L-shaped trench outside the north-west wall of this ward, which cut down below the thirteenth-century external ditch, more than confirmed the suspicion (**62**). A mass of stake-holes, indicating some sort of quite insubstantial structure, appeared at the base of the cutting: there was a quantity of ash and a series of baked clay layers associated with a simple cooking-oven. An archaeomagnetic date obtained from one of these layers, or superimposed hearths, was of AD 450–500 at the 68 per cent confidence level. This accords with the finding in the cutting of a surprising quantity (some 74 sherds) of Period II imported ware (B.i, B.ii, B.iv, B.v, Phocaean Red Slip, and five

63 *The outer wall-face of the Lower Ward, looking towards the Island. The wall, with a glacis below it, ditch, outer bank and (possibly) the dubious corner-tower foundations (lower left) are medieval. At the far end of the ditch, the paling-fence enclosed the CAU's 1986 cutting (photo: RCHME).*

untyped fabrics) and a few fragments of post-Roman glass.

The whole area of irregular cliff, between the Lower Ward and the valley floor (**63**) with the English Heritage shop and ticket-office, remains to be investigated. There are crude platforms that seem to have been improved, if not created, by human agency. The outcome of the short 1986 season was to confirm that Period II occupation does indeed extend below the mainland wards, inside the rampart.

1985: The Burnt Area
In the re-seeding operations carried out on the Island's Burnt Area in 1985, the CAU was asked to monitor the archaeological aspects; the burnt surface had to be lightly raked all over while the mixture of nutrient, grass-seed

and fresh water was applied. Finds thus made were plotted on an enlarged copy of the RCHME England survey plan. This cannot rank as an excavation, but it provided useful information; about 30 pieces of burnt pottery, either native Roman-period wares of Period II imports (B.i, B.iv and B.v amphorae were identified), were recovered. Added to the casual finds here from 1983 to 1985, they confirmed the noticeable absence of any medieval pottery. Various fragments of slate discs (pot lids?) and a few pieces of indeterminate slag were noticed.

1988: The Island
The Inner or Island Ward, with its modern footpath, can become muddy and waterlogged after heavy rain. A system of drains alongside the remains of the Great Hall, probably inserted by Kinsman in the 1860s, was being repaired in 1987. Certain finds made it desirable for the CAU to follow up the masons' diggings with a trial excavation, and at the same time to use the opportunity to produce, for the English Heritage archive, plans and elevation drawings both of the structures within the Inner Ward and of the Chapel.

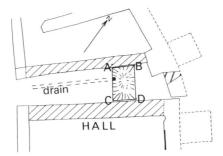

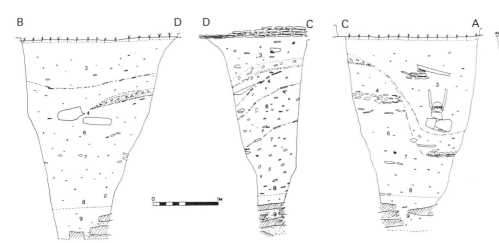

64 *The 1988 'Soakaway' cutting in the Inner Ward, immediately north of Earl Richard's thirteenth-century Hall. The four sections drawn, with great difficulty, by Nic Appleton-Fox show clear traces of successive tip-lines and, at the base, Period II walling-stones set in clay.*

The drains feed into a nineteenth-century soakaway pit, sunk just outside the supposed northern end of the Great Hall. Fragments of worked stone were now being found in disturbed ground here. When the CAU team, under Nic Appleton-Fox, opened a small cutting here, unexpectedly it failed to reach bedrock and indeed went down some 3m (10 ft). Interpretation of the results proved to be extremely interesting. In the 1930s (possibly in 1938), Radford's workforce had made several small cuttings immediately outside the curtain wall of the Inner Ward on a grassy strip above the slope where the 1918 'Cliff Fall' took place. These cuttings, probably 2 feet square but not now traceable on the ground, produced a good quantity of Period II imported ware, with some slag and fragments of bronze and – according to

the Finds Register – it seems they only went down about 18 in to 2 ft before encountering some kind of crude stone walling set in clay.

The 1988 'Soakaway' cutting, commencing at a much higher level inside the curtain wall, revealed at the bottom the surface of apparently similar unmortared walling, and at a horizon which must be the same as the base of the 1938 smaller cuttings outside, Radford's 'Site Z'. The sections on the four sides of the Soakaway cutting showed that, below the contemporary floor-level of Earl Richard's Hall, up to 3 m (10 ft) of ground had been infilled by a series of lateral dumpings containing such domestic debris as animal bones and a wide range of eroded Period II imported pottery (**64**). With a three-dimensional reconstruction of the entire Inner Ward of the 1230s, and also with the guidance of the still-visible section at its southern end, caused by successive minor falls into the neck and best seen across the chasm from the mainland Lower Ward, an interpretation of the evidence is now possible (p. 120). The natural hollow that holds the Lower Ward now forms the best candidate for the position of the Period II citadel's nucleus, probably

65 *The Island, eastern side: reconstructed two rooms of Site C, viewed from the south. Current excavations are on a barely-detectable terrace down the steep slope below the buildings (*photo: RCHME*).*

constructed on a set of two or three low-walled terraces.

1990: Site C

One, perhaps foreseeable and certainly desirable, outcome of the process of reinterpreting Radford's work in the 1930s was the pressure for renewed excavation on the Island, albeit on a minor scale. The reasons for this are numerous. There exists a genuine doubt that the post-Roman, Period II finds from Radford's sites A, B, C and F can safely be associated with the reconstructed and now-visible rectangular cells or walled foundations, many if not all of which can be considered as medieval (thirteenth century and possibly later). The discovery of much less substantial structures, in the Burnt Area where the associated finds are nearly all of Period II (with no medieval pottery at all) and from the 1986 work also outside the

mainland Lower Ward (with a stake-hole structure, and again predominantly Period II finds), must imply that Period II occupation did take place on sites A, B and the others, but at a lower level not recognized in the 1930s. The nature and extent of the stratigraphy (the successive layers of occupation debris and/or soil derived from vegetation) is still unknown. Because of the wholesale rebuilding in the Office of Works era, it is far from certain what a 'pure' thirteenth-century stone-walled hut or room would really look like. It would also be impossible to state with confidence that any Period II structures were not stone-walled, as well as turf-walled on stone footings; simply that none such has so far been recognized.

The 1985 survey identified a great many components – banks, platforms, large and small buildings below the turf – which, clearly, had not previously been recognized and certainly never excavated. A decision was made to examine an artificial terrace, apparently holding one or more hut-foundations, below and to the seaward (east) side of Radford's Site C, itself a small terrace with a complex of stone-walled foundations (**65**). The exercise, initiated by English Heritage as an aspect of adminis-

1 Surrounded by the sea on all sides – Tintagel Island with the Castle, from the north (WestAir).

2 *(Above)* Looking east along the coast from the Island: Barras Nose, a headland that has not yet been separated by a neck. Beyond, off Willapark headland, The Sisters, a dual rock that has become an island (RCHME).

3 *(Left)* A likely scene at Tintagel Haven in the sixth century. Cornish hands (modern) examine an African Red Slip dish from Carthage (ancient) (photo: Author).

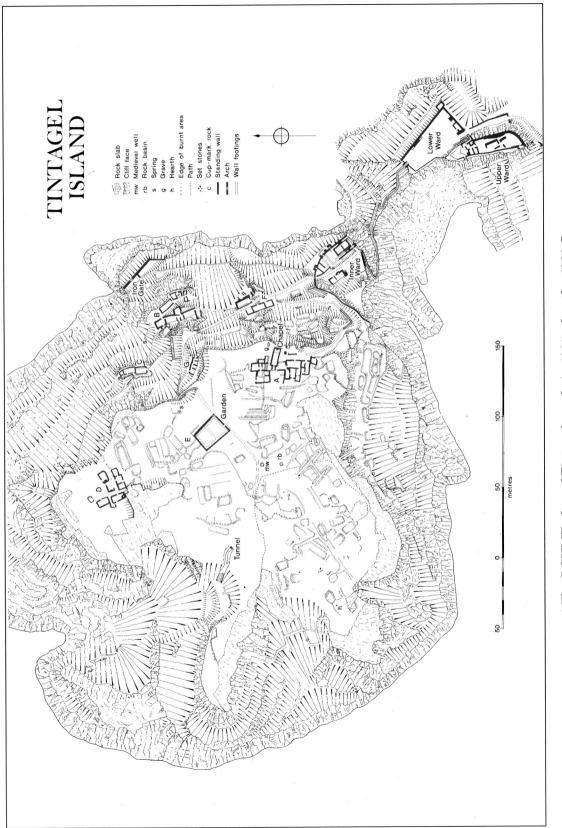

TINTAGEL ISLAND

⬡	Rock slab
▨	Cliff face
mw	Medieval well
rb	Rock basin
s	Spring
g	Grave
h	Hearth
⋯⋯	Edge of burnt area
⋯⋯⋯	Path
⋰	Set stones
c	Cup-mark rock
▬	Standing wall
‖	Arch
‖‖	Wall footings

Iron Gate

B

C

s

G

Chapel

g

A

Inner Ward

E

Garden

s

mw

rb

Tunnel

Lower Ward

Upper Ward

metres

50   0   50   100   150

4 The RCHME plan of Tintagel, made in 1985 after the 1983 fire.

5 King Arthur's Seat, on the southernmost edge of the Island; the 'Cups and Saucers' are visible on the floor of the Seat (photo: Author).

6 Aerial view of the Castle: landward wards and the Great Ditch, seen from the north-east (English Heritage).

7 The Island seen from King Arthur's Castle Hotel, showing the Haven and, centre right, the Iron Gate (English Heritage).

8 Aerial view of Tintagel Churchyard (Cornwall Archaeological Unit).

9 One of Veronica Whall's stained glass windows from the 1930s in King Arthur's Great Halls (Mr M. Godwin).

tering Tintagel as a Property in Care, has been entrusted to Professor Christopher Morris, University of Glasgow. Two short seasons (in the spring of 1990, and again in 1991) have already yielded highly significant results and have aroused great interest. Preliminary reports suggest that a 'keyhole' approach to any untouched part of the Island offers particular rewards. All the other, post-1980, work described above has had to be in the rescue, rather than research, category of excavation; reactions by CAU to archaeological needs arising in the first place out of non-archaeological disturbances like drainage repairs. The Site C operation has involved wet-sieving for plant remains, work at a pace permitting identification of numerous natural levels and minute-scale survey. The lower terrace does hold a structure of Period II, and it is apparently stone-walled, though with much finer walling than anything visible in the 1930s reconstructions.

1990–1: The 'Steps' Midden

Lastly, to bring this chronicle up to date, there are the finds made when a new flight of slate-faced, stone-packed steps was constructed to provide better access from the pathway just outside the Inner Ward's island-side entrance up to Site A and the Chapel. A whole string of rectangular foundations, some end to end and some laid out in near-parallel terraces down the slope, was noticed below Site A in the late 1970s and delineated in the subsequent survey. Close to, but outside, the Inner Ward, these look superficially medieval – an obvious location for castle-builders' lodgings – but the constant occurrence of sherds of Period II pottery exposed in the main pathway below them

implies that some kind of Period II activity or occupation was focused here. The lower part of the step-cutting intersected a rich deposit of burnt material and occupation debris with several hundred sherds and other small finds. Thanks to the sharp eye and meticulous recording of the mason who carried out the work (Mr Mike Rosewall) the general extent of the deposit could be plotted, and the Site C excavation team was able to deal with the exposure properly.

The entire thrust of the minor excavations listed here has been to confirm the non-monastic nature of the early occupation of Tintagel. Given the accumulation of new evidence it is difficult to see that any of it could refer to anything except massive, if irregular, use of the Island for secular purposes at times within the fifth and sixth centuries AD. None of it is conclusive. These have not been extensive area diggings, and none of these various trenches or cuttings has exposed more than about .001 per cent of the available ground. The best that could be claimed is that we now have a very fair idea of where, on the Island, area excavation (of a kind involving a budget far beyond anything likely to be available) might answer outstanding questions. And questions certainly remain – we are in the position of folk who clear a table-top, unpack a box holding a thousand-piece jigsaw puzzle and find that only about a hundred pieces have actually been included in it. Because of this predicament, no definitive account of early Tintagel is yet possible and this book cannot pretend to be anything better than an interim statement. However, the next two chapters must reflect an attempt to reduce all the information into a model of Tintagel's past.

6

Models for the moment – Roman and post-Roman

Tintagel in the Roman period – Period I

Cornwall in Roman times formed the western part of the large administrative region known as the *civitas Dumnoniorum*, the canton of the people whom the Romans knew as the Dumnonii. It was an outlying peninsula in a province forming part of the Roman empire. To say that in the nineteenth century Wei-hai-wei and Witu similarly formed outlying parts of the British empire is not to adduce a precise parallel – who now remembers Witu? – but it makes the point that Cornwall, the land beyond the river Tamar, was remote, under-populated, uncivilized, and therefore also unimportant until, during the third century, the local tin-streaming industry attracted attention. There had been a brief military subjugation in the first century and it is possible that, as with the Northumbrian moors today, the area was occasionally used for military training and practice-camps.

Five inscribed Roman 'milestones' or route-markers have been found in Cornwall, two of them from the Tintagel neighbourhood. None refers to a conventionally-built Roman road in the sense of Watling Street or the *Via Appia*, but they must imply a degree of official and centralized recognition of certain routes, going purposefully from A to B. Of the Tintagel pair, a granite pillar with the names of Gallus and Volusianus (AD 251–3) was found at Trethevy (see **6**), a hamlet on the present coastal road between Tintagel and Boscastle, and now stands in a Trethevy market-garden. The larger local-slate slab (see **5**) first spotted (in oblique sunlight) in 1889 built into the lychgate stile of Tintagel churchyard, is preserved inside the church; it dates to the reign of Licinius (AD 308–24). It is not known where it was found

but, since there is an ample supply of slate slabs all around the churchyard, there would have been no point in fetching it from any distance and it must have been discovered close by.

Tracing the courses of lost Roman roads in the British countryside is a time-honoured pursuit, often a productive and successful one, but difficult to follow in Cornwall. Here there are no detailed road maps until Joel Gascoyne's (1699) and the only longer-than-a-mile straight alignments seem to be the post-1800 turnpikes and the new roads to serve mines, laid out across waste country. On the other hand the whole pattern of parish churches and early medieval farm-settlements in north Cornwall suggests that, by the eleventh and twelfth centuries, and therefore arguably rather before this, a customary trackway did come down the coastal belt – not actually along the edge of the cliffs but a little further inland where the land forms a shelf and where the numerous valleys can be skirted before they deepen into ravines. (From Boscastle going west to Tintagel, this is the line of the present B 3263 road.) Both the Tintagel milestones could relate to it. The likely function for any such Late Roman route would have been commercial rather than administrative (and certainly not military). But where, in that case, was the route heading?

The Romans compiled and used itineraries, simple lists of major roads fanning out from centres that named all the places in order and indicated the distance in Roman miles, *millia* (the *mille passuum* of about 1500 m (5000 ft)), between each. Certain such itineraries survive, often in garbled form. Remnants of some relating to Britain together with a mass of other geographical information appear in a text compiled soon after AD 700 at Ravenna in Italy

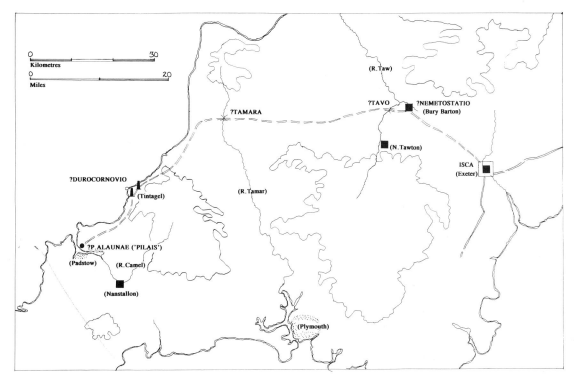

66 *Map of west Devon and east Cornwall, with a possible Roman route to the Camel estuary. Modern names are in brackets.*

(the 'Ravenna Cosmography'). The anonymous compiler's British source was a lost road-map, but the degree of distortion and corruption of individual names in making use of this was considerable. One section relates to the south-west, where the key location is *Scadu namo-rum* (= *Isca Dumnoniorum*, Roman Exeter). It is just possible that a sequence does represent a Late Roman route running into Cornwall. The forms are *Giano . Eltabo . Elconis . Nemetotacio . Tamaris . Purocoronavis . Pilais*. Given that a few of these names are recognizable and that the initial *El-* is pretty obviously an error for *Fl-* (*flumen*, 'river') the most recent authors have restored the sequence (if sequence it really is) as: *Glano . Fl(umen) Tavo . Fl(umen) Cenio . Nemeto statio . Tamara . Durocornovio . ???*. In this, *Tavo* is a crossing at the north Devon river Taw, *Cenio* another unidentified crossing, and *Nemeto statio* is a 'station', an establishment such as a tax-gathering post, either at North Tawton or now preferably the excavated site at

Bury Barton near Lapford (a small fort). *Tamara* is the river Tamar, either for a ford or for some place of that name at a crossing (**66**).

Are the next two names in Cornwall? Of *Pilais*, described by the editors as 'meaningless as it stands, and must be corrupt', the present writer has suspected that it may represent *P* (= *portus* 'harbour, landing-place') followed as in other such names by that of a river, in the genitive case. If we are on the north coast, is *-ilais* for a lost *-alaunae*; *Alauna* being a fair guess at a Romano-Celtic name for the river Camel? Its older name (*c*.1200) was *Alan*, and there are no less than eight examples of *Alauna* – meaning uncertain – as a river-name in Roman Britain. The Camel estuary with Padstow on its west bank is, apart from Hayle (St Ives Bay) further west, the only safe landing-port of any size on the north Cornish coast; there is also a certain amount of purely archaeological evidence to show that it was so used both in Late Roman and post-Roman times. One relevant third–fourth-century site lies buried on the *east* bank, below the St Enodoc sandhills; and now surface finds from another, on the *west* bank but north of Padstow, include the rim of a Phocaean Red Slip

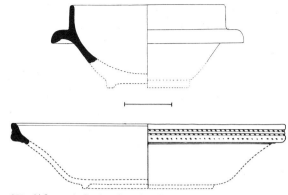

67 *(Above) Oxford red colour-coated flanged bowl (Young: form C.51.1), fourth century, Tintagel Island. (Below) Roulette-stamped rim of Phocaean Red Slip Form 3 dish, fifth – sixth century, a recent surface find from a site just north of Padstow. (*Drawn by Carl Thorpe; scale bar, 5 cm.*)*

Form 3 dish, identical to many others recovered from Tintagel (**67**).

This leaves us with **Durocornovio*, the Ravenna *Purocoronavis*; it means 'the *duro* of the Cornovii', who were the inhabitants of what became Cornwall. The element **duro* means, loosely, some kind of fort or walled town and it appears in the names of quite large places like *Durobrivae*, Water Newton, and *Durovernum Cantiacorum*, Roman Canterbury. Whether any such place existed somewhere in the north-east quarter of Cornwall, and at some point between a Tamar crossing and the Camel estuary, is a mystery; certainly no conventional settlement has been located. Whether in an un-Romanized district **duro-* could be used (as *din-* ('Tin-'), from British **dūnum*, seems to have been used) for a natural stronghold employed for any kind of settlement is equally unresolved. But it is worth inclusion here, in case this happens to have been the place-name of a small Late Roman establishment at Tintagel.

The archaeological evidence for this is still only tentative. So far, no structure excavated on the Island – and this comment covers Radford's 1935 Site A finding (p. 60) – can be put forward as a Roman-period settlement, native-peasant or otherwise. Yet we cannot dismiss several hundred sherds, mostly from the Island and still being found in the minor post-1980 excavations, which if from any other site in Cornwall or Devon would be interpreted for

what they look like. They represent jars, flanged bowls and platters, local products made on a slow wheel, their forms clearly influenced by coarse Roman wares and conventionally dated to the third–fourth centuries AD.

There are two possible explanations here. One relies on *survival*; there may have been no occupation of the Island at all before the fifth century, and this pottery – cheap, easily made, easily broken – represents 'remnant stock' or was even still being produced long after 400 somewhere in the south-west. The other explanation would deny this on several grounds, mainly that where (in the west of Cornwall) we do have locally-made pottery on native sites of the fifth and sixth centuries it is of a different kind, recognizably so. What slightly tips the balance is the record of other finds. The Tintagel material includes sherds of a non-local Oxford red colour-coated ware (see **67**) that must be seen as fourth century, and certainly reached Late Roman Cornwall; there are other pieces from sites in the Land's End. There is also the curious tale of the coins. In the short 1956 season, Radford's re-sectioning of the Great Ditch of which records are sadly lost (p. 59), the workmen found wedged among some rocks – exactly where is not known, but in the vicinity of the Upper Ward crag or the outcrops east of the Lower Ward walling – a hard dried object they took to be a fossil. This was given to a Tintagel lad who was interested in such items. Advised by the village chemist he soaked it in a bucket of a glycol for a time, and eventually it turned out to be (from his detailed description) a little Roman-type drawstring leather purse. It contained ten low-denomination bronze coins, recently re-examined; this hoard is now on show in a private minerals and fossils museum at Tintagel. The coins range in date from Tetricus I (AD 270–3) to Constantius II (337–61) and this is someone's private nest-egg, shoved into a hidey-hole not before the second half of the fourth century.

Putting this together, and remembering the presences of the two milestones, a kind of conclusion can be reached; though no claim is made for it beyond saying that it simply forms a model for the moment. In the period from the mid-third to late fourth centuries, metal extraction yielding small ingots of streamed tin – an Imperial monopoly – at the streams all around the northern side of Bodmin Moor may be linked to a route skirting the Moor and going to a natural harbour opposite Padstow. Eastward continuation of this route (beyond the Tamar) towards Exeter may be reflected in what can be made out from the Ravenna list of places. Minor finds suggest, at face-value, that either the Island or the landward area of the later Castle (or both; but before any Great Ditch was constructed) formed the scene of third–fourth-century habitation. Whether such an establishment had any quasi-official standing, like a taxation or ingot-marking point, we cannot say; nor is it known if it had a name that figured in any itinerary and, if so, whether that name was 'Durocornovium'. Years ago R.G. Collingwood wrote a paper on Cornwall's Roman milestones and the scant evidence for ancient tracks that might represent routes employed in connection with a Late Roman tin industry; but he confessed himself at a loss when it came to explaining the positions of the Trethevy and Tintagel churchyard milestones. All that can be said is that he wrote before the 1933–8 excavations, which hardly clarify the picture. It is not yet safe to go beyond the suggestion, mainly from archaeological finds, that there *was* a Period I at Tintagel. Its nature continues to be elusive.

Post-Roman Tintagel – Period II

Setting aside for the moment various past interpretations, the historical explanations for what took place at Tintagel during the archaeologically-defined Period II, there are several basic obstacles in the way of defining a fresh model. During the fifty-odd years when the place was claimed to house an Early Christian monastery, a date-span corresponding to this book's Period II was derived from (*a*) the most likely age of any such monastery; i.e. from the later fifth century to a time before the first Viking raids, say 450 to 750; and (*b*) the dating, increasingly refined as precise identifications became possible, of the imported Mediterranean pottery. Occupation of the Island by a monastic community whose size had to correspond to a large number of buildings was implicitly continuous throughout. The awkward question – if Tintagel then was as important as the quantity and quality of finds, and the sheer size of the foundation, would suggest, why did this leave no trace in any historical record? – was invariably side-stepped.

If the monastery is deconstructed, the sole indication of date is that provided by the pottery. Some (not all) of the imported wares can be dated from North African, Aegean and Eastern Mediterranean contexts, and also because certain types (like B.i and B.ii) did develop known differences of shape and detail over a long period. On the assumptions that things such as fine red-ware dishes and bowls were mass-produced, stocked in warehouses and generally readily available in markets, and that any assemblage of pottery vessels (if regarded as a unity) must be dated to its latest known components, it would be quite proper to make the following statement. *All* the imported Mediterranean and North African pottery, of all kinds, so far found at Tintagel arrived on one occasion only – hundreds of jars and dishes, in a single sailing-vessel that berthed for a summer afternoon against the Iron Rocks landing. But when? This author, if faced with a firing-squad, would be happy to pick out (and defend) an absolute date like AD 535 for this event; nor does it matter that some of the North African red-slip bowls included as space-fillers represent forms probably current from the 470s (**colour plate 3**).

Clearly, and particularly so since the 1985 re-survey, this could not explain all the evidence for occupation – disentangling Period II structures (with some difficulty) from those of Period IV – or the implied stratigraphy. But the principal difference between the 'monastic' model and what will be suggested below is that Period II occupation may never have been continuous. It has already been pointed out that, save possibly for an all-year peasant caretaker, the pre-Castle Island was not then and is not now a place for the winter months if anywhere more sheltered, inland and with better natural resources, is available. That refers only to a single calendar year. But it is now suggested, on a longer perspective, that between about 450 and about 625 the Island was only inhabited periodically and occupation may have been solely during summer months. Continuation of occupation into the seventh century is for the moment excluded because of the absence of any evidence for it. If the suggestion is to be taken seriously, any interpretation has to reconcile what has been found with a set of historical and social circumstances, within which such sporadic use can be imagined.

No valid model of past happenings can stray outside deductions and inferences drawn from the available evidence – supposed facts that can be freely checked. For instance the Period II occupants may have grazed goats on the Island but, as we possess no goat horn-cores or indisputable goat bones, the speculation would be pointless. Consider in summary what *is* known about Period II at Tintagel. The place, with its neck or saddle linking mainland to Island, is to some degree a natural strongpoint. It was rendered even better protected by the construction of a ditch-and-rampart line across the only point of landward access; it was turned into a true fortification. The barrier was landward, not seaward; and the Island was unusual in possessing a kind of natural wharf, the Iron Gate rocks, linked by a pathway up to the most sheltered spot, the hollow subsequently marked by the medieval Inner Ward. Yet the Island's Period II remains, insofar as these are identifiable, cannot be put forward as those of some fortified coastal village. The place is too restricted, and too vulnerable to gales and to salt-laden spray; the soil-cover is meagre and shallow, the water supply limited. Nor would the archaeological finds support such an interpretation. Imported pottery aside, the early sherds (whether Period II or from Period I), discarded stone tools, remains of domestic animals and general rubbish-deposits do not occur in anything approaching the density or the quantity that would have arisen during a couple of hundred years of continuous occupation. It would be a counsel of despair to argue that all this was thrown over the cliff-edge, because inspection reveals that on a detailed scale the Island has no such convenient cliff-edges.

The imported vessels – amphorae, fine-ware dishes, coarse wares – clearly arrived by ship, in one or many shipments, directly or indirectly from the Mediterranean, and were probably off-landed at the Iron Gate rocks. Unless this is supposed to have been a surprise gift from a shipmaster who had risked his vessel, his capital, his crew and himself to come a very long way indeed, the material has to be interpreted as the evidence for one half of a two-way exchange. In that case, there will be a presumption that any such eventuality had been arranged somehow in advance, and therefore that long-distance communication had been established. Since there is no commodity that occurs naturally on the Island, or immediately at Tintagel, which could appropriately be exchanged for containers by the hundred full of wine, olive oil or anything else, let alone handsome and shiny red plates from Tunisia or the Byzantine world, the questions that have to be asked are not only *what* were these imports exchanged for; but also how did the occupants of the Island manage to acquire and to amass on-site whatever goods formed their contribution to this commercial exchange?

Questions that arise from a consideration of a great mass of hard archaeological finds, things that anyone is free to inspect, handle and analyse, are not in quite the same category as questions that may be given shape by considering later literary or mythical attributions. It could, however, then be wondered why, in the *Tristan* cycle, Tintagel figures as a stronghold of 'King Mark' – as Oliver Padel points out, a person from pan-Celtic folklore, not some attested historical ruler – and why Geoffrey of Monmouth chose to include Tintagel as a citadel of Gorlois Duke of Cornwall (this, independently of Arthur's magical conception there). If this is a pointer to the kind of stories that Cornish people were telling in the twelfth, eleventh or earlier centuries, how long before that had such 'stronghold of the ancient rulers of Cornwall' tales been circulating? Where (finally) in all this is there even the faintest hint of an exclusively Christian establishment, like a major monastery?

If such questions are examined – and they are all questions that anyone who thinks hard about the problems of Tintagel's past may well want to consider – a picture begins to take firmer shape. It may be one to which Celticists and early medieval historians, as well as analytical archaeologists, can give sharper focus and added colour. In the collapse of any belief that a monastery existed here, a number of then-fashionable explanations were proposed, but for the most part rejected. One, that Tintagel Island formed a trading-post or emporium where imports were received, stored and thence sold or exchanged over a wider region falls prey to commonsense: the geographical position is too marginal. There are other and more obvious harbours; one would not expect trade-goods retained at the point of importation to outnumber so markedly occurrences of similar goods within a radius of 10, 20 or 50 miles. (Cornwall in Period II never had a monetary economy.) Another theory, that all the imports represent votive offerings made at some major religious shrine or temple, must also be dismissed. Where, in the field archaeology, is there any structure remotely likely to represent a temple, and by the sixth century what particular religious faith would such an improbable focus signify? Why should traders from Antioch or Alexandria or even Bordeaux wish to make votive deposits on the coast of Cornwall? Suggestions of an idiosyncratic fortified town, or of a defended farming settlement, have (as shown above) no support at all from the known archaeology or the natural situation.

A post-Roman citadel

For the currently preferred model, the Island, and a small part of the adjoining mainland, in Period II is seen as a secular citadel based in a natural stronghold, with direct access by sea; its landward defence-work is real enough, but so large as to possess tones of ostentation, and outward emphasis upon status and power. This citadel was not, and was not intended to be, a place of permanent occupation. Hence its temporary inhabitants would expect to be victualled from outside, and to supplement the Island watering-points through fresh water from the valley stream below. Like the making of the Great Ditch and its rampart, and the levelling of small platforms around the sloping edges of the Island's plateau top, supply-arrangements on this scale imply control of human labour; and control, too, of the lives of many over a surrounding region. Similarly the evidence for the direct (or indirect) importation of exotic Mediterranean goods – at an appropriate price and seemingly on a scale not yet known to be matched elsewhere in western Britain – should imply centralization of wealth, or capital products, also created by human labour. At the centre of the web, the Island in Period II, archaeological interpretation of what has been found through survey and excavation and the location of finds may still be imprecise, but it points already to the occasional presence of a large, rather than small, number of people, not all accommodated at the same standard.

There is more than one mode of putting all the implications into plain language. Theoretically-inclined scholars, wishing perhaps to avoid committing themselves to over-concrete wording, would (and do) use such phrases as *high-status defensive secular settlement, centres of tribute* and *hierarchies of sites.* These are not so much cases of a private jargon

in part borrowed from other disciplines, as a kind of short-hand for concepts whose full explanation would take up many pages. The writer, who does not expect to be around if and when any radically different new model for Period II Tintagel emerges on purely archaeological grounds, can afford to be specific. Tintagel Island, certainly in the period AD 475 to 550 and probably for longer, served as a stronghold for the post-Roman kings of Dumnonia. The place was used only seasonally or periodically, as part of an irregular sequence of visitations and/or in connection with particular dynastic happenings. It was a point to which not only food and water, and perhaps certain materials for craftsmen, but also goods required for foreign trade were brought under a system of enforced obligations. By the sixth century such a ruling caste was Christian. There is probably no Period II Christian sacred site on the Island, because the contemporary 'sacred space' underlies Tintagel's parish churchyard.

Whatever the Island was called in fifth–sixth-century Late British speech (not necessarily 'Tintagel'), and whoever the individual kings or potentates may have been, some knowledge of the place's Period II role and status was maintained through oral tradition or folk-memory. The belief that such a periodic use of the Island ceased by the seventh century is to some degree drawn from negative evidence; notably the absence of at least two sorts of known seventh-century domestic pottery (the imported, Gaulish, Class E range; the locally-produced grass-marked platters and cooking-pots) that occur widely elsewhere in Cornwall and Scilly. A phase of virtual desertion – in the Island's chronology, the gap between Periods II and III – should not have eroded a continuing tradition, if such beliefs led to the (Period III) linking of Tintagel with legendary heroes like 'King Mark' and *dux* Gorlois. Reverting to Early Christian monasticism, the denial of such a role to the Island does not mean that early monastic communities did not exist in sixth-century Cornwall. In fact the nearest monastery to Tintagel would have been *Landocco*, at or near the parish church of St Kew (about 16 km (10 miles) to the south), and the nearest *visible* monastery on the island of Lundy (about 56 km (35 miles) to the north) – both were founded about 500 with the impetus in both cases coming from coastal South Wales.

Post-Roman kings

The phrase 'post-Roman kings of Dumnonia' calls for explanation. Unfortunately they have to remain unnamed. Even if it were not contended that Tintagel's Arthurian connection is due to Geoffrey of Monmouth's twelfth-century fancy, 'kings' would exclude the hypothetical *Arthur* of post-Roman times, who was never claimed as more than a general or war-leader and whose activities are often regarded as having been set in northern England and southern Scotland.

The Roman-period *civitas*, the administrative and fiscal region of the south-west known as Dumnonia, covered Cornwall and Scilly, Devon, and part of Somerset. In Wales and in parts of England and southern Scotland, the end of Roman domination in the fifth century AD was followed – not necessarily at once – by the appearance of notional states small and large, kingdoms or political groupings controlled by certain extended families. Most such people, then or later, claimed a descent from Late Roman emperors and usurpers or notable Roman figures, and in most cases the nature of kingship (under whatever term, Latin or British) was not a father-to-son succession but a system in which successors were chosen from an eligible kin-group, the common descendants of some earlier ruler. The choice was usually narrowed through battle casualties and assassination of relatives.

Two features make it difficult to produce anything corresponding to neat regnal lists. There *are* surviving records of the names of regional kings, and they do occur in the form of regnal successions and not as genealogies; but these were compiled by bards and historians, centuries later, from extremely fragmentary sources (with fictional padding) and the brief list for the kingdom of Dumnonia is notoriously suspect. Again, these post-Roman British rulers are rarely if ever associated with named localities or single centres of rule. The whole idea of the native kingdoms possessing fixed capitals, towns or fortresses, would be a misleading anachronism. A typical king with his family, relatives, dependants, resident hostages, officials and court-followers, and a private militia or war-band – in all, probably between a hundred and three hundred souls at least – moved around with his cumbersome entourage; at least, when not busy with inter-tribal campaigning or in repelling invaders and

raiders. The reason to keep on the move, as Thomas Charles-Edwards points out, is fairly obvious: 'no large household could stay in one place for more than a few weeks without a long-distance trade in all essential foodstuffs'. This may not have applied to the many, but generally unrecorded, local petty sub-kings who may have chosen to reoccupy older native earthworks; but it can be assumed that it held good for the monarchs of more extensive states. The solution was *itineration*, an existence deliberately on the move, visiting various places in turn where enforced hospitality (food renders from the populace) met such needs. It was, in effect, easier to take the whole court to the food, rather than to reside permanently at a central place and bring all sustenance inwards to the court from an ever-diminishing neighbourhood source.

Dumnonia, in our Period II, from the Isles of Scilly to the Somerset Levels was some 320 km (200 miles) long. There are only suspicions as to where likely points in any such sustenance-circuit may have been, or how great a demand was made on them. It is possible that some place-names in medieval Cornwall with the prefix *lys* ('court, administrative centre, palace'; these meanings are approximate only) refer to this system. Helstone in Trigg, now a hamlet on the Wadebridge to Camelford road and only 11 km (7 miles) south-south-east of Tintagel Island, is (like the larger Helston town in west Cornwall) Cornish *hen* + *lys* + English *ton* 'settlement'. *Hen* means 'old, ancient' in the sense of 'former, obsolete, abandoned'. It is probable that early locations within a kingship itineration disappeared centuries ago under large manorial estates or medieval market-boroughs. As for the kings of Dumnonia, there is not much point in trawling through a catalogue of names. From the writer Gildas we know that a *Constantinus*, Constantine, was king of Dumnonia in the early to middle sixth century. Names of a few others, like the first of two kings called *Gereint*, are historically just acceptable, but not acceptably dated.

The evidence for post-Roman buildings

Can this hypothetical model be applied to the Island's Period II remains (if identifiable as such) and finds? The initial fit has to address the internal hierarchy of the site itself, the ranking of the remains by size or desirability or

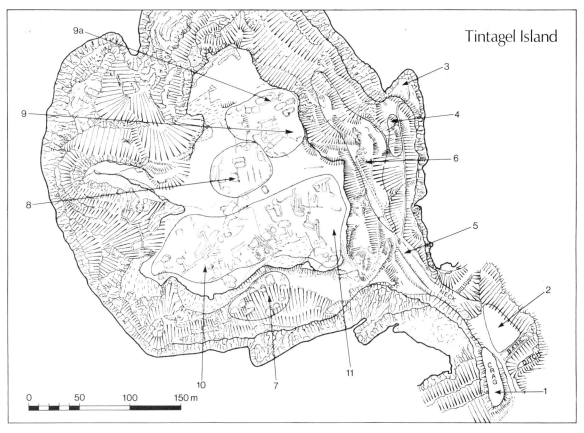

68 *A hypothetical model of the internal organization of Tintagel as a post-Roman citadel (using the base-map of the RCHME survey with known or suspected medieval features blanked out).*

1 *strongpoint (Upper Ward);*
2 *occupied fore-part;*
3 *landing (Iron Gate), with 4 any defences;*
5 *terraced nucleus (below the Inner Ward);*
6 *higher-status occupation;*
7 *separate (specialized?) occupation (South Terrace);*
8 *permanent 'caretaker'?;*
9 *with 9a ('Hall'), another specialized area;*
10 *turf-walled bivouacs, war-band?;*
11 *uncertain, eastward extension of 10 and/or south-western extension of 6.*

context. If we think of a few months' residence in a summer, the temporary dwelling of a king is likely to have been 'grander' (provided we know what that means) than the temporary dwellings of those who did the dirty work for the cooks, or trudged up and down with leather buckets to fetch water. This exercise may resemble a put-it-together game rather than any controlled historical reconstruction, but a useful starting-point would be to take the 1985 RCHME survey, to blank out all the features known to be fully medieval (like the Castle) or suspected to belong to Period IV (like the larger and more regular groups of rectilinear walling), and to see what is left (**68**). The results of minor post-1980 diggings, and (to some extent) the known distributions of certain small finds, give additional aid.

The approach has recently been suggested by Professor Leslie Alcock, whose prolonged study (with his wife Elizabeth) of all such royal centres in post-Roman Britain greatly expands the field of enquiry. Tintagel Island may be large, prominent and in a Cornish context rather on its own, but as a Period II stronghold it goes with many other sites, frequently also coastal, and particularly in Scotland. A whole body of

69 *Members of the Cornwall Archaeological Society, on a 1988 outing, indicate the discernible foundations of the 'hall' just south of Site D* (photo: author).

annalistic references to the sieges, defendings, burnings and captures of such citadels, mainly in the seventh and eighth centuries, may reveal a deplorable side of contemporary society, but it is extremely convincing witness that such places *were* being occupied by rulers or their subordinates. Physical irregularities of the defended interiors, excavated remains, evidence of shorter or longer habitation and the uneven recovery of significant small finds all suggest to Alcock that, in theory, patterns of some conventional or graded use and allotment of internal space might be noticed. Is this applicable at Tintagel?

Beginning at the landward side, the medieval Upper Ward is defined by a roughly oval walled enclosure perched on a natural crag. It commands the thirteenth-century Lower Ward entrance, which was almost certainly built on the site of the Period II entrance through the inner rampart; it also commands a splendid view down the whole course of the Great Ditch; and despite tidying-up and constant erosion by visitors' feet the interior of the Upper Ward has

produced a fair quantity of Period II imported pottery (as surface finds). It is therefore difficult *not* to see this as a sentry-point or manned lookout in Period II; it can also be questioned whether any of the rougher walling (irregular blocks) at the base of the thirteenth-century ramparting had been there since the sixth century. From the 1986 excavations, it is known that there was Period II occupation in this landward sector (p. 62), and possibly the area now taken up by the Lower Ward held, as it presumably did in the thirteenth century, facilities for horses to be stabled or tethered.

Crossing the saddle that may once have stood high above today's neck (but, since it no longer exists, with no further comment) we reach the Island. The potential use of the Iron Gate rocks as a Period II landing-place has been discussed (p. 43), and one or more of the just-visible overgrown platforms in the slope above the Iron Gate may prove to contain Period II occupation. The principal riddle in postulating an occasional kingly use of the Island is the whereabouts of anything that might be interpreted as such a ruler's hall, or some lodging larger and grander than any other. Surface indications may not inform us. On the RCHME survey plan, there is a rectangular foundation (with rounded corners and perhaps a hint of internal divisions) (**69**), unexcavated but which can still

70 *The natural hollow occupied by the Inner Ward, on the south-east corner of the Island* (photo: RCHME*)*.

partly be detected below the turf, just next to Radford's Site D. This foundation is externally about 23 m (75 ft) long. It is the largest single unexamined structure so far noticed, and one to which the term 'hall' could well be applied. However, it is on the most exposed part of the Island, and also lies well outside the known spread of Period II finds – virtually no pottery was found at Site D. The 'hall', or whatever it is, should perhaps thus be seen as a medieval item; a store or barn, belonging (like the Tunnel as a larder) to the Castle.

Since no other suitable building can be found through surface traces, the solution may be that the Period II nucleus, the living-quarters at the summit of the social hierarchy, are concealed. And in fact the brief 1988 excavation, together with the marked emphasis in the distribution of Period II imported pottery, suggests that the structures in question were where they would be expected – in the most sheltered, physically most favourable, nook: the natural hollow filled by the Inner Ward and the Great Hall (**70**). The indication is that the post-Roman nucleus, which may have been in the form of stone-walled rooms stepped down over two or three shallow terraces, lies *underneath* Earl Richard's Great Hall – several metres below the Hall's floor – and the evidence for this will be given in the following chapter.

Within the Burnt Area, most of the southern half of the Island's top, the traces exposed by the 1983 fire were of small, roughly square or stubbily rectangular, structures. These had slate footings that probably supported low turf walls, retained in place by upright stakes (the points where stakes were hammered in can be seen in one case, a row of little impressions in the slate bedrock (**71**)). These would have had temporary roofs – a few beams, brushwood and turf or even hides. It looks as if a large group of such bivouacs extended from the south-east corner, right across to site A, and there were more on the western part of the South Terrace (below 'King Arthur's Seat', p. 75). There is some Period II pottery from this sector, though far less than from the Inner Ward, or sites B, C and F. It is therefore tempting to see such remnants as those of a Period II camp-site, summer quarters for those used to roughing it; in other words, the military followers or war-band. How long a life such insubstantial constructions had is uncertain, but there is a good parallel from Iceland where the annual national assembly, *Althing*, took place at the spot called Thingvellir ('Plains of Assembly').

71 *The Island, Burnt Area. Impressions of points of wooden stakes originally driven through turf walling, on the exposed bedrock slate. The main row (at least 6) is 2 m (6½ ft) long, with an average interval of 38 cm (15 in); note traces of shorter inner row, with intervals of 27 cm (11 in). White garden labels point to the impressions (*photo: author*).*

Scattered booths, or *búðir*, simple structures of turf and stone that for a seafaring nation could be roofed with spars and sails, stood there awaiting their annual temporary use.

The entire east-facing sloping side of the Island, starting at the Inner Ward hollow and then continuing along to Site C, possesses all the year round the greatest shelter from the wind, and catches any sunlight from early morn to mid-afternoon. Here, if anywhere, one would look for superior Period II accommodation, spaced out on natural ledges or man-improved platforms and connected by narrow pathways. In social terms, it should have been preferentially used by the upper reaches of a post-Roman retinue. Here, too, is by far the largest concentration of all kinds of Period II imported pottery, notably the fine-ware African and eastern Mediterranean dishes. Below the reconstructed 'monastic cells' of the 1930s, the joined-up rectangular rooms that it has been suggested are really Period IV lodgings for the Castle's masons and labourers, may lie older and smaller structures. Precisely such an example, and it is indeed neatly stone-walled, is now under excavation by Professor Christopher Morris and his team on the lower terrace or platform of Site C. If Radford's Site B is examined closely to try to make sense of where walls have been rebuilt for display and where older straight joints and butted ends are still visible, there seem to be other instances of small, almost square and rounded-corner, rooms or cells (**72**) that can be differentiated from the long rectangular Period IV buildings. The records of the 1930s work do not allow a precise knowledge of how, if at all, the numerous finds of Period II pottery were contextually or stratigraphically linked to what look like Period II stone-walled chambers; but the renewed examination at Site C arouses suspicion that precisely such links did exist.

The last component in this model of the Island's interior is to be found in the centre of the plateau. It is hardly ever noticed (**73**). Here, and here alone, is a small group of four or five stumpy little rectangular foundations, with traces of small linear cultivation-plots between them. The whole is contained in a slight hollow, affording shelter from the north and northwest. The term 'caretaker' sounds banal for a Dark Age royal citadel, but it may be precisely that: a citadel-keeper's humble home, a permanent presence on the Island independent of brief, spaced-out, occupation on a larger scale.

Nothing in this model amounts to more than a hypothesis. It does nevertheless put forward an explanation for what can be seen, taking into account the recent observations that structures likely to be referable to Period II are not all of the same kind. Until and unless (say) the Burnt Area is excavated – not a difficult task, because the vegetation cover here is scanty and the soil above slate bedrock is generally shallow (10 to 20 cm or 4 to 5 in) – we are stuck with models, instead of the kind of detailed information now coming from the Site C excavation.

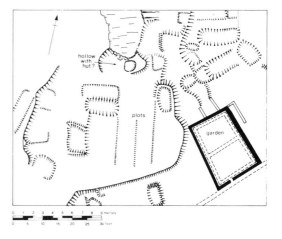

72 *A 'room', rebuilt in the 1930s, on the south-west corner of Site B, seen from above. Is this in fact a small post-Roman structure like those in the Burnt Area, and on the lower terrace of Site C?* (photo: author.)

73 *A 'caretaker's' establishment? Features in the centre of the Island, including a small well-sheltered hut in a hollow, parallel plots, other foundations and a surrounding bank.*

The imported pottery

Perceptions must widen, and yet another set of models be put forward, when it comes to explaining the presence of the fifth- and sixth-century Mediterranean imports. Some of the imported wares have already been mentioned, and a bald summary will suffice. The following types are represented at Tintagel: there are North African Red Slip dishes, broad-rimmed platters and flange-rim bowls, from the Carthage area (**colour plate 3**); and also Phocaean red-slip bowls (all the so-called Form 3) from near the Aegean coast of modern Turkey. Possibly fifty or so of each have now been recognized. The amphorae begin with B.i, or Carthage LR (= Late Roman) 2. These are found in huge numbers in the eastern Mediterranean; they may not all have come from, or have been filled for shipment at, the same places, but mainland Greece, Crete and the wine-producing Greek islands are probably involved. B.ii amphorae, Carthage LR1, are known to have been manufactured at numerous kiln-sites along the coastal plain of Cilicia, south-east Turkey. The small B.iv dark red-brown micaceous ware amphorae (**74**) (Carthage LR3) originate at or near Sardis (Sardes) in western Turkey. The very large B.v vessels, tall cylindrical things with short handles and a restricted neck, closely resemble a known Tunisian kind (Africana II 'Grande'),

but examination of minerals in the clay rules this out and points to an unlocated East Mediterranean source. Then there are dozens of instances of untyped or unclassified amphorae, sometimes a single pot, sometimes three or four, and also wheelmade coarse wares – versions of cooking-pots, jars and skillets, the likely equipment of a ship's galley. Most of these last are of fabrics of East Mediterranean type, but there may be a few North African pots among them. Some of the PRSW (Phocaean Red Slip Ware) Form 3 dishes have stamped ornament, including small expanded-arm Christian crosses, on their inner bases (**75**). Mixed up with the pottery are a few tiny pieces of thin glass, fragments from drinking-vessels; it is not clear if these are also from the Mediterranean (similar glass was mass-produced in Egypt) or from somewhere in Gaul, and it also not clear whether the occasional grey-fabric bowl or mortarium sherd at Tintagel is a local (Exeter?) Late Roman wheel-made product or yet another known import, Class D, which was produced somewhere in Atlantic Gaul. The overall impression of the Mediterranean material is that it was gathered piece-meal from a number of ports, and makes up the kind of cargo that might be expected with a vessel trading on its owner's behalf.

There have been (we now know) many instances going back to the 1920s of single sherds, or a handful, indicating anything from

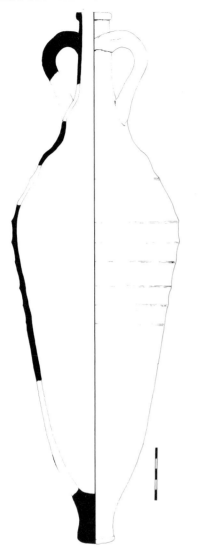

to 423, since these may very well have been payments to the tin-workers of the time; and a few cases where small finds of post-Roman character have been discovered in tin-streaming deposits. The hypothesis is that ingot tin was supplied, in the later fifth and sixth centuries, to centres of power (or centres of tribute) like Tintagel, and that a small proportion of the luxury imported goods found its way back to the suppliers. The reasons to suppose this really arise from elimination of most other possibilities. There is no cause to think that post-Roman Cornwall produced a surplus of foodstuffs, specialized items of leather and textiles, or particular animals like hunting-dogs. It is unlikely that the rulers of Dumnonia were in the business of selling battle-captives to foreigners as slaves. At comparable post-Roman citadels, notably in Scotland and Ireland, evidence often occurs for the presence and output of master-craftsmen, especially metalworkers producing personal ornaments; this is an expected aspect of High Life at the time and clearly one that could figure in external trading. Tintagel, from the

75 *Tintagel: fragments of Phocaean Red Slip Form 3 dishes with impressed stamps of crosses on the inner base. (*Below*) Mediterranean instances of such stamps (reduced), types 71 and 72 in Dr John Hayes's catalogue. (Scale bar, 5 cm.)*

74 *Reconstructed drawing, section and profile, of a B.iv amphora from Tintagel; note the narrow neck, tiny handles and 'corrugated' body surface. (Scale bar, 5 cm.)*

one to a dozen various imported pots being found at excavated sites in Cornwall, the Isles of Scilly and south Devon. Some of these sites are large and possibly important, like reused hillforts. Others are simply post-Roman homesteads. Many of the sites lie inland, away from the coastline. A distribution-map of the finds on their own tells little, but it may have more meaning when plotted against the valleys worked for streamed tin in Late Roman times (**76**); the pattern of Roman coin-hoards, AD 253

1930s work and now from smaller recent diggings, can show just enough hints in the shape of droplets or chunks of smelted bronze, metallic slag, perhaps pieces of crucibles, to suggest that metalworking did take place here in Period II – but nothing is known of the finished products.

Tin on the other hand, an essential component of the alloy bronze, does not occur widely;

was in Roman and later times known to be available from the alluvial deposits in Cornwall and Devon; and was both valuable and in demand throughout the Late Classical world. The combined distribution-map can thus suggest that the occurrence of Mediterranean imports accords with the notion of, at least, a trading-voyage that firstly reached the Isles of Scilly and then proceeded up the north coast of Dumnonia. The cargo may here and there have been depleted, to the extent of an amphora or two, for supplies (in Scilly, where there is no tin, perhaps a sheep and fresh water when making landfall from the European coast) but the principal goal was one or more centres where the bulk of the goods might be exchanged for a substantial amount of handy tin ingots. (These are heavy, but convenient; some known examples are about the size and shape of a large Cornish pasty.) Tintagel was the leading centre, one whose lords were in a

76 Cornwall: centres of power, tribute and exchange in the fifth and sixth centuries? Key: 1 centres (Tintagel, Camel estuary, Carnsew). 2 Imported Mediterranean pottery, relative quantities. 3 Tin-streams worked in antiquity, with (4) post-Roman finds from them. 5 Coin-hoards with dates of depositions AD 253–432. The radiating arcs are drawn (distances from centres) at 15 and 30 miles (24 and 48 km).

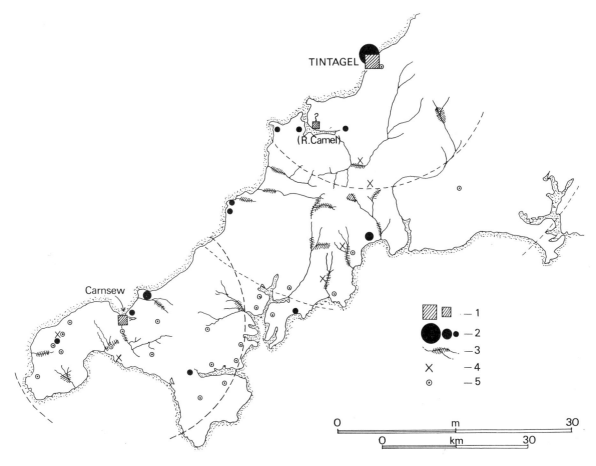

position to exact tribute over much of Cornwall. It looks as if there may have been another and minor centre to the west, and Carnsew – a small coastal fortlet at Hayle, in St Ives bay – is an unexcavated candidate for this. On **76** the arcs are drawn with radii of 15 and 30 miles, distances equivalent to one day's, and two days', travel by foot or with a pack animal.

Conversely the *outwards* diffusion of little gifts by the rulers to favoured subjects – here the odd dish, there an amphora or two – is implied by the stray finds. Amphorae had probably already been emptied and were merely exotic objects. This is actually consistent with the main hypothesis. In the west, pieces of a B.i amphora from the reused stone fortress of Chun Castle were associated with sixth-century native ware, a crude furnace and an actual block of smelted tin. The small settlement at Gwithian west of Hayle (producing about half-a-dozen amphorae as fragments, B.i and B.ii) was an estuarine farm at the outflow of two noted tin-streaming valleys. The substantial 'round' or circular fortification at Trethurgy near St Austell, apparently still inhabited in the fifth and sixth centuries and similarly yielding fragments of amphorae, also produced a tin ingot.

What the evidence cannot tell is how many such trading-trips took place. Forgetting the minimal view argued earlier (p. 85), the overall British and Irish distribution suggests at least four separate ventures, one going as far north as the mouth of the river Clyde in western Scotland, and these may be the tip of a forgotten iceberg. The trip, or many trips, or sea-route, up the north coast of Cornwall really belongs to a larger map (**77**) because the route continued to the Severn estuary. It is becoming clear that another coastal focus, having features in common with Tintagel, existed at the hillfort of Cadbury near Congresbury on the Somerset littoral, approached by the then-tidal river Yeo. It would have been a most suitable centre of power and tribute linked to the pewter-ware industry of Mendip, if this was still functioning around AD 450–500, which is a possibility.

The hypothesis cannot answer all the puzzles but for the moment it offers a best-fit for the known evidence – the mechanism of a seaborne trade is simplified, points of import identified, diffusion inland is explained and tin is put forward as the most likely medium in the

exchange. Late Classical maritime trading in the Mediterranean took many forms, with practices stretching back over centuries. It was hazardous – the sailing-season was short, April to September – and a direct sailing all the way to Britain and Ireland would have been an investment at risk. In British waters a short day's sail, beaching or tying up offshore at night, would be consistent with the known spread of contact-points indicated on the maps. It is possible that the whole trade was *not* direct, and that goods from far away had firstly been landed and sold at some European Atlantic entrepôt in Portugal, Spain or western France (Bordeaux, the ancient *Burdigala*, is such a place). Presumably exchanges were negotiated in Latin as a common tongue. Presumably, too, one such voyage could deliver notice of a future one – so-and-so intends to arrive about Midsummer next year.

Ceremonies at Tintagel

This leads to another imponderable, archaeologically at the very core of attempts to interpret Tintagel's Period II occupation. How often was the place so used? Can we guess at specific occasions, beyond the usefulness of Tintagel as one within a whole circuit of suitable temporary residences, when it may have been visited? Two such do suggest themselves. Going back to all those Island-top features described in Chapter 3, King Arthur's Footprint (p. 49) may have been rather more than something at which Victorian tourists could goggle. It is to be found on a flat slate ridge, forming the highest point on the Island. From here, there is a panoramic view of miles of Cornwall, east and west, and one also looks straight across at Tintagel church, itself standing on the highest point of the Glebe Cliff opposite (**78**). The feature is an indentation in the worn slate surface, apparently improved by human handiwork, and unevenly oval. It will accommodate a human foot, even a foot in a stout boot. The Footprint cannot as it stands be dated, any more than the cup-marks (the 'Cups' or 'Saucers', p. 49) inside the nearby King Arthur's Seat. But it would be difficult to argue that it was fully prehistoric, BC and not AD, in

77 *Mediterranean imports in post-Roman western Britain and Ireland (known to 1989); the distribution suggests at least four voyages – a minimalist view.*

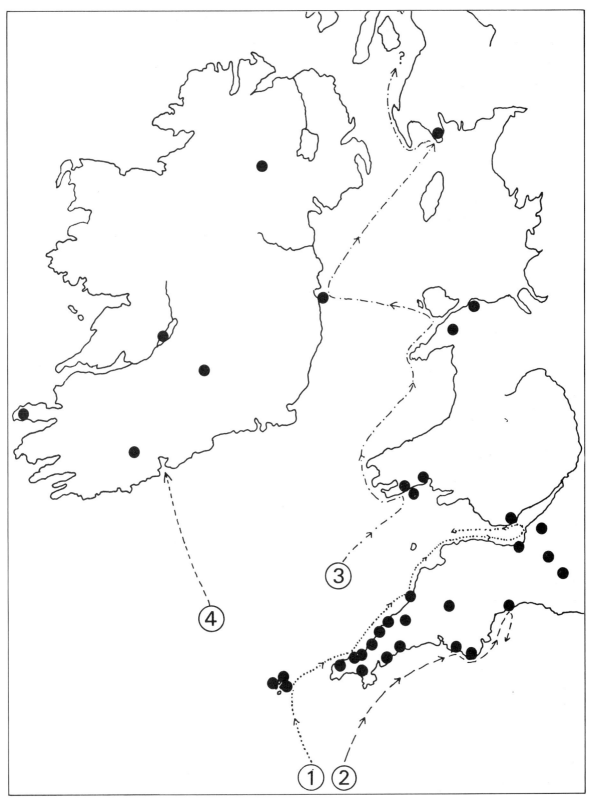

78 *Sacred site from secular site; seen from the top of the Island, Tintagel's ancient church dominates the slightly higher Glebe Cliff* (photo: RCHME).

the total absence of any other evidence for prehistoric activity.

On the other hand, it does belong to the world of the non-Romanized Celts. In places in Ireland and western Scotland with its Isles, similar single or double impressions of foot-marks in the living rock are associated with inauguration ceremonies – the ritual crowning of a king, the elevation of a tribal or clan chieftain. These continued well into medieval times. The symbolism is ancient, going back at least to Iron Age times. Placing a foot in such a mark denotes the assumption of rightful sovereignty over the surrounding territory (and in Freudian or Frazerian interpretations, this derives from a symbolic act in which a king undergoes a sacred wedding with the personified Land). There is no echo of the custom in Cornish folklore, but this may be so only because it was a very early one.

It can be wondered, therefore, if the occasions when the Dumnonian ruler and his court – or any other major chieftain in the post-Roman south-west – came to Tintagel included public recognition of a king as replacing his dead predecessor, and whether this rock-marking figured in the ceremonies. In turn, this shunts

other questions to the front. Does it perhaps mean that independently of (presumably also before) the use of the Island as an occasional Period II seat it possessed some special significance? Was this an aspect of the place as a natural phenomenon, sacred in isolation? If the Footprint dates from the Roman period and belonged to the Celtic peoples of the Cornovii or Dumnonii, irrespective of their incorporation in Roman *Britannia*, should, among possible interpretations of the Island's Roman period finds (p. 85), that of a small Romano-Celtic shrine with a resident custodian be also included? It is wholly possible that among the dozens of surveyed, but unexcavated, foundations all over the Island's top there could lurk such a modest construction. In that case the sacred character of the Island, however commemorated, might indeed have been formulated in prehistory. This is not to agree with those who automatically see the Tunnel (p. 46) as a ritual passage, a holy souterrain of pre-Roman days, or who argue for such a prehistoric attribution because of the subsequent connection with the (massively irrelevant) Arthur. But when examples of such alternative views are examined (Chapter 8), it is only fair to admit that some of them may be making a valid point for the wrong reasons.

The inauguration of a new post-Roman king was a celebration focusing on the living, and a fresh life. Standing beside the Footprint, there is a parallel outlook, concerned with the dead. The handful of human burials, in graves some of which were more rock-cut than others, reported from the Island seem to have included at least one (judging from an old *Western Morning News* photograph) that was, like dozens of others found along Cornwall's coasts, for a fairly recent drowned mariner. (Until an Act of 1808 ordaining churchyard burials promoted by the Cornishman Davies Gilbert, PRS and MP for Bodmin, these unfortunates were summarily buried near the spots where the sea cast them aground.) There is no evidence for a cemetery or any formal concentrated point for burials, ancient, monastic or otherwise, anywhere on the Island or within the mainland wards. And since 1990 there is also no point in looking for one. The research excavations within the northern sector of Tintagel parish churchyard have shown that Christian burials here began at least as early as the sixth century, took place during most of the post-Roman Period II on the Island, and that archaeologically the Island (as the secular centre) and the churchyard-area (as the Christian sacred space) are intimately linked. However, though Period II has been defined as ending (or reaching a pause in the record) some time after AD 600, no such equivalent break occurs in the churchyard's chronology and the whole topic is therefore more suitably described in the next chapter, where it forms a natural prelude to the consideration of Period III. In conclusion it may be noted that the rock ridge of the Footprint, if linked to early royal inaugurations, also commanded the Island's best view of what may have been an early royal burial-ground. The occasions of deaths may also have had some influence in deciding when, and for how long, the citadel on the Island was deemed suitable for occupation.

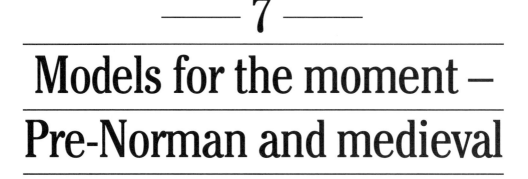

Models for the moment – Pre-Norman and medieval

Tintagel churchyard

The parish churchyard of Tintagel is extensive – it has been enlarged several times in recent centuries – and about a half-mile from the village. It stands at the edge of a chequerboard of fields enclosed by drystone slate walls, some probably medieval. Glebe Cliff, the open cliff heathland fortunately owned by the National Trust, slopes away in front of the churchyard and, just as the church is visible from the Footprint ridge on the Island, so the most striking view of the Island occurs from a little way beyond the churchyard wall.

Notes of previous discoveries there included in A.C. Canner's parish history, local memories, visible features and (in 1986) a proper survey made by RCHME (**79**) all supported the belief, subsequently shown to be justified, that this is another major archaeological site going back to Period II, if not also to Period I; and a site that would have to be taken into account in formulating any model for the Island itself. Superficially, the spatial separation between the parish church and Tintagel village should be linked to the fact that architecturally the church begins in the early twelfth century, whereas the linear emphasis of the village (Fore Street) suggests development alongside a trackway to the Castle, and therefore not before the early thirteenth century. This does not explain the choice of the church's siting in the first place and the real explanations are rather more complicated. By 1988 it was possible to put forward in print a hypothetical sequence for the churchyard starting in the equivalent of Period II.

Given this baseline for future exploration, it was a happy chance indeed that Mobil North Sea Limited – a company involved in North Sea natural gas extraction, and with a fine record of support for cultural activities in Scotland – offered to sponsor an appropriate excavation marking the launch of a new platform called *Camelot*. A generously broad interpretation of the adjective 'Arthurian' led the party looking for an excavation to sponsor, straight into the arms of the party looking for sponsorship for their planned excavation. The two seasons, 1990 and 1991, so far undertaken at Tintagel churchyard have been blessed with success in all possible ways. The partnership has been happy and smooth, the publicity enormous, the results prolific, and in 1990 Mobil won the year's British Archaeological Award for the most imaginative sponsorship of an archaeological project. The illustrated report on the 1990 season broke all known records with a circulation of some 9000 copies, and in 1991 Mobil also supported an educational programme that allowed groups of children from all over Cornwall to visit the work and share in the excitement. For the people who matter most, the parishioners, the excavations that they enthusiastically backed (and permitted) reinforced long-held ideas as to the antiquity and significance of Tintagel in Cornwall's early history. For archaeologists, this was a rare example where a detailed model of a large and relevant site could be formulated, adequate funding made available, and the model could be tested by a research excavation. The inevitable outcome, that unpredicted discoveries now demand still further investigation, is just one of those things.

The advent of Christianity

In any region of Britain and Ireland the advent of the Christian faith meant more, speaking

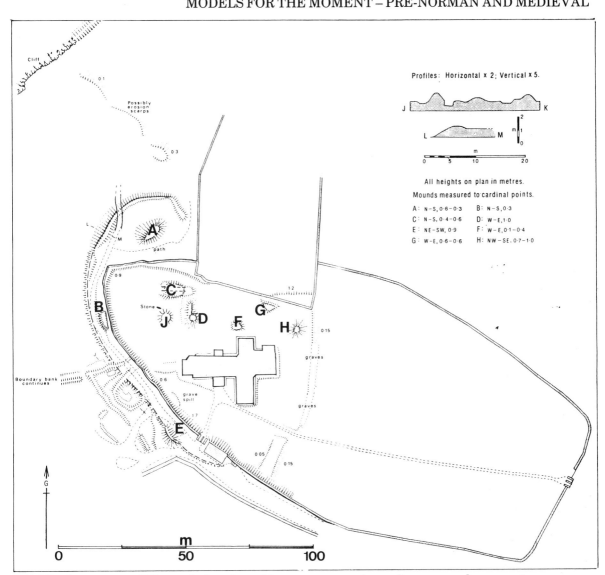

79 *The first survey of Tintagel churchyard by the RCHME, 1986. Of the lettered mounds,* B *is now regarded as part of the enclosure-bank and* E *(sectioned in 1990) an isolated deposit of rubble. (See also colour plate 8.)*

historically and archaeologically, than the adoption of what became a universal religion in place of localized or specialized pagan beliefs. 'Advent' here could be defined as a band of time past, broad or narrow, at the start of which a given area with its inhabitants knew nothing of Christianity and at the end of which Christianity had become the dominant religion, supported exclusively by a ruling class. History suggests the time-band, the whole process of

conversion, often covered one or two generations – say ten to fifty years. Its historical identification in each instance comes from written records, usually retrospective ones exaggerating the roles played by missionaries, martyrs and miraculous demonstrations. There is an equally informative *archaeological* identification because the practice of Christianity leads to types of burial, graves and funeral-monuments, buildings for worship (churches), field-monuments (cemetery enclosures, monastic enclosures) and specifically Christian art on stone and other materials.

In fourth-century Roman Britain, Christianity was a minority faith. It was not everywhere wiped out in the social and economic turmoils that we imagine happened in the fifth century, nor in the later fifth and sixth centuries by the expanding settlements of the pagan Anglo-Saxons. However, the known extent of fourth-century Christianity barely touches Dumnonia (there are faint signs from *Isca*, Exeter, the only sizeable Roman town in the *civitas* of the Dumnonii). In Cornwall and Scilly there are indications of Christians immediately around St Ives bay, where the Hayle estuary is the main western landfall along the northern coast; but such signs, from about 450, are very localized and may have been due to seaborne contact with some part of Christian Gaul (north-west France).

For all of north-east Cornwall, including Tintagel with its hinterland, around the north and south of Bodmin Moor into the Tamar valley and then eastward into the South Hams of Devon, the advent of Christianity can be approximately placed at AD 480–530; no earlier. This innovation was probably not the work of missionaries (as we now understand that term), nor was it fully accidental. It would be safer to call it incidental. Would-be settlers from south-west and south-central Wales, some of them probably aristocrats with followers, came over to Cornwall and took up land. By 480–500 most if not all of these immigrants were themselves Christians, and there were priests among them. The natives adopted the new faith from their invaders – a reverse of a process that can be discerned from parts of England where invaders may have received Christianity from the natives.

The first-named Dumnonian king, Constantine in the period 500–550, was upbraided by Gildas for his sinful life in wording that shows him as a nominal Christian. He was probably named in imitation of Constantine I, the Great, the first Christian Roman emperor (died 337). Nothing is known of his life and career, geographically; it is impossible to say if this man ever used Tintagel Island or indeed if in the sixth century all of Dumnonia had a single ruler. But it may be safe to believe that any postulated kings or sub-kings after 500, periodically on the Island, were together with their extended families and superior followers all Christian, nominal or devout.

A paradoxical side in a religion that emphasizes the Divine conduct of life here below and the promise of Life Eternal to follow is that the earliest Christian archaeology is almost entirely concerned with *death*. As a detectable new fashion, Christian burial involved inhumation (burial of the corpse in the ground) and not cremation; absence of grave-goods; orientation or alignment of the body east–west, head to the west; and, since burial near that of some prominent saint or martyr gave greater assurance of participation in the Resurrection, Christian graves are found grouped together with increasing frequency. As a secondary stage such groupings are contained in an enclosed, consecrated, cemetery.

The area of Tintagel parish churchyard includes just such an early cemetery, contemporary with the Island's post-Roman Period II. It is not certain, since the evidence comes only from rumour, whether Period I – the Roman centuries – is also represented, but it seems possible that the choice of this particular spot as the first Christian burial ground may have followed directly its use as an open, pre-Christian, burying area. A large stone cist, a slate 'box' with a boulder over it, was reputedly destroyed in the field just south of the churchyard in the 1950s. A late Iron Age and native Roman-period cist cemetery is not unlikely, but again little is known about Period I, or prehistoric, life on the whole coastal shelf now dominated by Tintagel village. A thousand years of enclosure and intensive farming have rubbed out almost all the field-archaeology. What the 1990–1 work has shown is that, potentially, the churchyard has been in use without any real break from some time after AD 500 until today. That situation may not be unique but the chance to confirm it through excavation very rarely arises. Both seasons of excavation, directed by Jacqueline Nowakowski for a consortium of Cornwall Archaeological Unit and the Institute of Cornish Studies (University of Exeter), are fully described in the published reports; what is included here is therefore a summary.

Tintagel churchyard in the post-Roman period

Tintagel churchyard exhibits at least six detectable phases, of which the first two (sixth, seventh, possibly also eighth century) overlap with Period II at the Island (**80**). In the area investigated, a small part inside the present northern wall, the Early Christian burials took place in both slate-lined cist graves and unlined body-length hollows or 'dug graves'. In 1990

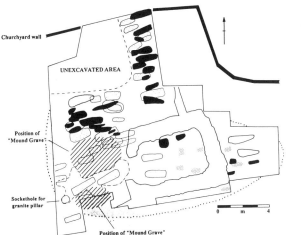

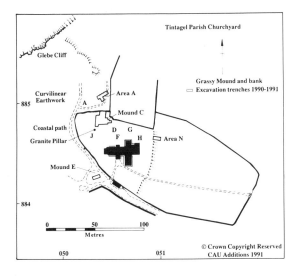

- - - - Edge of 1942 trench
───── Edge of excavation trench 1990 - 1991
∴∴∴ Area of Mound C
☐ Phases I and II burials - Early Christian
☐ Phase III burials and ruin - Pre - Conquest
■ Phases IV and V burials - Medieval
▨ Phase VI burials - Post Medieval
▨ Position of "Mound Grave" found in 1990

and dried, proved to be from a B.ii amphora. In due course, other sherds of other kinds of amphorae (B.i, B.iv, B.v) were found, some in subsequently-disturbed contexts, but enough to show that quite a few vessels had been brought to this cemetery (**81**). It would, in a classic phrase, multiply hypotheses beyond necessity to imagine anything except that these came from the Island in Period II. Why, and how? Refreshments for grave-diggers is a far less attractive explanation than that these, perhaps refilled with local beer or mead, formed part and parcel (with whatever was baked in the graveside fires) of a funeral meal, conducted beside a burial either at the time of interment or on some subsequent anniversary.

Also of great interest was the discovery, for the first time in the south-west, of numerous slate slabs, large and small, marked with knife-point crosses, or in some cases with designs of circles scratched with simple iron dividers used compass-fashion (and here we are reminded of the enigmatic craftsmen of the Island in Period II, since these are craftsmen's tools known from other sites). 'Primary cross-marked slabs' or 'primary grave-markers' occur widely in sixth-century Ireland, the Isle of Man, western and northern Scotland and occasionally in Wales (**82**). The Christian cross, even as two scratched lines at right-angles, is a symbol not generally employed in Britain and Ireland before the early sixth century.

Now all of this was unexpected, and quite new. Given the proximity of the Island and the supposition that its temporary Post-Roman, Period II residents, a percentage of whom might be expected to die – and at that time,

the granite pillar some 1.75 m (6 ft) high, unearthed by Mr Arundell and the airmen in 1942 (p. 64) and left on the grass, was re-erected, but in 1991 the socket-hole where it had originally stood in the sixth century, on the old land surface nearly 2 m (6½ ft) below today's grass, was found. Some of the earliest graves seem to have been aligned on it. On the old surface, just south-west of this socket-hole, traces of burning were noticed; an open-air fire, fragments of mature oak yielding a radiocarbon date (GU-2798) which, calibrated, centres on AD 403 – consistent with its having been burnt a century, or a century and a half, later. Compacted into the burnt clay and charcoal were sherds which, when carefully winkled out

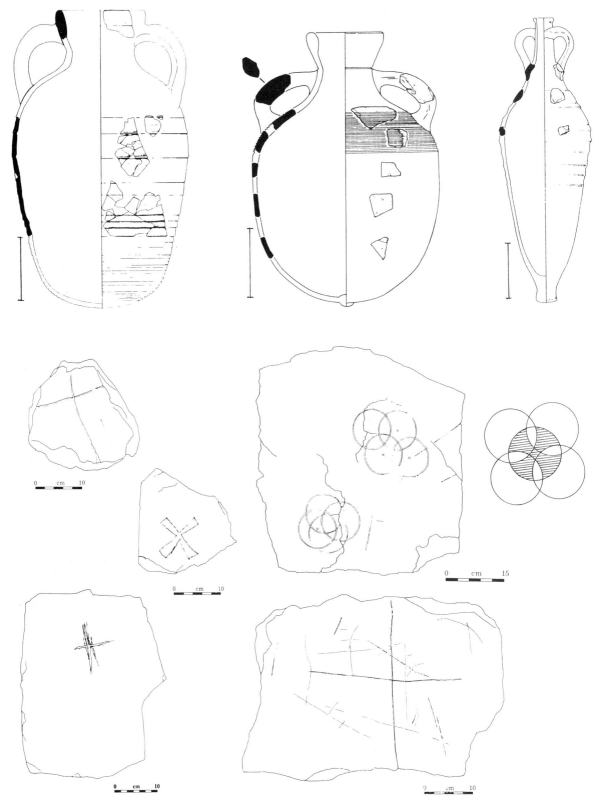

life-expectation was not high and infant mortality was common – over a period of some months' occupation, this Early Christian burial-ground can be assumed to hold the remains of Island communities. The use of cross-marked stones to mark individual graves (some are the covering slabs of cist-graves, some may be separate markers) is a native custom; the plain, or outlined, crosses may be copied from initial designs in Christian manuscripts or even from the stamps found on the inner bases of imported red-slip pottery dishes. Compass-drawn circles, disposed in patterns, can be used to display what are called 'crosses of arcs' (see **82**). This, and perhaps also the funerary custom of the ritual graveside meal, is Continental (European) rather than Insular (British and Irish). It suggests ideas brought in along the same general route as the imported luxuries.

Because of reported discoveries and chance findings during grave-digging, agriculture and hedge-removal over the last 60 years, it is known that the area of oriented cist-graves here extends rather further than the present churchyard. It suggests that the burial ground during the sixth century, if not later, was open and not enclosed, and must have been used for the Christian dead of the whole district. However, there are remains, notably outside and north-west of the present churchyard, of a low bank of earth and stones enclosing a roughly oval area as much as 150 m (c. 500 ft) north-west to south-east. This was sectioned in 1990 and 1991. Trying to date such a feature by trial cuttings is a problem – feasible in theory, if one is lucky enough to encounter clear pre-bank and post-bank datable finds. In practice there is an extremely small chance of doing this. The

earthwork is clearly older than any part of the twelfth-century walled churchyard, the shape of the latter being influenced by the line of the earthwork (on which in part it sits), and the entrance – or the only detectable entrance – is on the *north*, linked by an old hollow trackway to the landward part of the Castle. In the post-Roman period this would have led to the entrance over the Great Ditch. A single sherd of African Red Slip pottery was found in the roughly-paved entrance area. Provisionally, then, the enclosure is seen as a secondary (later sixth century?) modification of the Christian burial-area, defining its most important part; as such, it goes with a hundred or more similar ovoid and circular banked and walled enclosures (*lans*) to be found in Cornwall, many of them underlying the siting of present-day parish churchyards.

What the churchyard excavations have not yet established is until how late these superimposed burials, cists or dug graves, of the Early Christian phase (Period II) continued (**83**). A much larger area would have to be opened – this is neither possible, nor contemplated – to check the matter. In the 1986 survey, various low grass-covered mounds could be defined, generally north and north-west of the actual church; most are within the present walled churchyard, but since one (Mound A) lies just outside it, the inference is that the mounds are in fact contained within the older enclosure. This might imply that they, too, are of Period II, and Arundell's 1942 trench through Mound C did at first seem to support such an implication. Total excavation of Mound C in 1991 showed it to be, in general, both complicated and later; a continuing and planned accumulation of soil and clay, with a stone-wall spine, seemingly centred over early graves placed near the once-upright granite pillar. What this may mean is a puzzle, as is the nature of the other mounds, one or two of which may represent dumps from medieval and early modern rebuildings of the church, avoided for grave-digging and exaggerated in outline by further dumping.

81 (Above left) *Tintagel churchyard: imported pottery, almost certainly brought over from the Island.* (Left) *B.ii amphora – fragments from a small area of burning, 1990.* (Centre) *B.i and* (Right), *B.iv from the 1991 season.* (Reconstructions drawn by Carl Thorpe. *Scale bars, all 10 cm.)*

82 (Left) *Tintagel churchyard: primary cross-incised slates* (drawn by Carl Thorpe). *The two larger* (right) *are covering-slabs for graves. The diagram* (top right) *shows how a correct placing of compass-drawn circles can produce a 'cross of arcs'* (shaded portion).

Tintagel in Late Pre-Conquest and Norman Times – Period III

As indicated in Chapter 1, this is a time-division of convenience, embracing a whole series of events that are archaeologically distinctive or have left remains. Period III ends

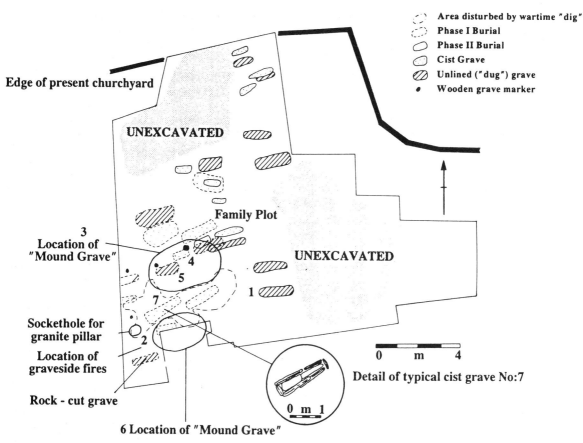

Legend:
- Area disturbed by wartime "dig"
- Phase I Burial
- Phase II Burial
- Cist Grave
- Unlined ("dug") grave
- • Wooden grave marker

Edge of present churchyard

UNEXCAVATED

UNEXCAVATED

Family Plot

3 Location of "Mound Grave"

Sockethole for granite pillar

Location of graveside fires

Rock - cut grave

6 Location of "Mound Grave"

Detail of typical cist grave No:7

0   m   1

0   m   4

83 *Tintagel churchyard, 1991: the lowest levels, Phases I and II, with Early Christian graves (fifth–seventh centuries).* (*Drawn by Jacqueline Nowakowski.*)

with the building of the Castle (about 1230–6) because that particular happening must denote the start of a Period IV.

Though the duration of use of the Island as a post-Roman citadel (Period II) cannot be shown to extend beyond the late sixth or early seventh century, and the next detectable event – the building or conversion of the Chapel – is probably in the eleventh century, Period III covers also the churchyard and the whole Tintagel district. The hundred, or hundred and fifty, years before the Norman Conquest of 1066 (with Cornwall subjugated by William's forces in the early 1070s) is conveniently described as *late pre-Conquest*. At Tintagel this is manifest almost entirely in ecclesiastical archaeology and, before turning to the hard evidence, it will be helpful to provide something of the background.

Throughout England, the parish system (essentially as known today) involves the partition of the whole land regardless of lay ownership into ecclesiastical units: parishes. A parish is a closely-defined tract, large or small, with a principal church under the cure of an incumbent (rector or vicar) who may or may not be resident. It gives *outward*, at a church designed for public worship, spiritual care – the incumbent's main task – and the necessary offices: the Mass and services for baptism, marriage and burial. It receives *inward* the whole network of requisite support: tithes on land or produce, which in the 1830s were commuted to cash payments, various fees in relation to the offices, and any income from the glebe, the estate of land with which a church was originally endowed. (The glebe at Tintagel seems to have been intended as 50 statute acres.) This admirably simple mechanism, now unfortunately prey to changes, served England for the best part of nine centuries. For long, it was a truism of historical thinking that the entire parochial network as known today came into being shortly after the Norman Conquest – by about 1100; and, in Cornwall, that it could not be traced before the early twelfth century. Such a view would (at Tintagel, in particular) accord with the observation that the construction of the large parish church began about 1120–40.

Research in the last decade, however – something that can be summed up in the title of a recent influential volume, *Pastoral Care Before the Parish* – upsets this entirely. From the evidence of hundreds of pre-Conquest Anglo-Saxon charters and documentary descriptions, as well as the results of landscape studies, archaeology of church buildings, and even well-targeted excavation, it is certain that the parish system was not some vast nationwide innovation at all. After the Normans, it had to be accommodated to a parallel network of boroughs, chartered market-centres and manors (many of them representing pre-Norman estates) but in earlier centuries a more relevant link was with the patterns of settlement and population. In the ninth to eleventh centuries – and in certain parts, possibly as early as the end of the eighth century – a system of pastoral care centred on the existence of what can be conveniently called *minsters*. A minster (Old English *mynster* – this comes from Latin *monasterium* 'monastery') was an important central church, very likely having other buildings, such as dwellings, attached, from which a team of priests served a 'parish' or area that would be the equivalent of anything up to six or ten modern parishes. By the tenth century, this was supplemented through the rise of private or estate churches built by large land-owners and staffed with resident priests. The outward element of the minster system cannot have been very different from that of the twelfth-century parochial system; the inward element must have comprised a version of tithes and fees but relied heavily on royal, communal or private endowments, frequently described as funds to ensure the forgiveness of sins, certainty of salvation, or constant prayers for the donors. For a whole range of reasons, still under exploration, the period from the tenth to the twelfth century – late pre-Conquest and early Norman – saw, everywhere, a major campaign of building enlarged stone churches.

In the 1930s it is doubtful if anyone would have supposed that the sequence just outlined applied to Cornwall. Pre-Norman Cornwall was envisaged as a peninsula spiritually dominated by monasteries; and 'monasteries' meant, on the whole, places founded in the remote past (the fifth, sixth or seventh century) by individual missionary saints arriving from Ireland or Wales. It also meant establishments of a Celtic appearance, typified by the former interpretation of the remains on the Island. Subsequent parish churches were hardly ever demonstrably rooted in this monastic system. Today a far greater connection is envisaged; partly because a rigorous examination can pin-point only a quite small number of such monasteries in Cornwall (many smaller examples may have been a local version of estate churches), and partly because by the late ninth century these monastic houses were in fact starting to function as minsters on the wider, southern English, model.

The importance of work at Tintagel – excavation, fieldwork and fresh evaluations of finds and monuments – since 1988 has been to show that the minster model is applicable to this part of Cornwall. Its emergence can define a Period III, starting in the first half of the tenth century; and it is possible that what holds good here may hold good for the rest of Cornwall (though the outcome of a projected study in 1993–4 must be awaited). In the 1990 churchyard diggings, the lower part of a broad east–west wall composed of slate blocks, quartz and volcanic greenstone was encountered just east of Arundell's 1942 trench. At the time it was taken to be an earlier (twelfth–thirteenth-century) north wall of the churchyard and its abrupt eastward end was assumed to be one side of a wide north entrance-gap. When in 1991 a much larger area had been opened, this wall was seen to be a foundation-course, in a trench over a metre wide, of a rectangular structure whose longer axis ran east–west (**84**). The western end, in part destroyed by the 1942 trenching, had been modified with some secondary building; but the original structure would have been externally at least 7.5 m long, and 5.5 m across north–south (about 25 by 18 ft overall). The compacted rubble fill of the interior, into which several post-medieval burials had been inserted, was deliberately not excavated down to the contemporary floor.

The interpretation of this structure as an earlier church, one whose actual walls (of neatly-laid slates in a clay mortar, as one or

84 *Tintagel churchyard, 1991. Incomplete foundation-course, assumed to be that of a late pre-Norman church. (Scale bar, 4 m.)* (Drawn by Jacqueline Nowakowski.)

two surviving traces showed) had been robbed for reuse, cannot be certain until the interior has been fully explored. Its size and shape, context, orientation and resemblance to certain other buildings make this the most likely answer. Nor is this all. Stones used for its foundation-course involved slight varieties of the local greenstone, and some of these blocks showed dressing and chamfering; they had come from another and earlier building with formal details. Among them were two remarkable pieces (also of greenstone, but not of the immediate local outcrop, the now-filled quarry known as Nute's Pit 180 m (600 ft) south-east of the church) which belong to a baptismal font.

The font is of the 'tub' variety, with small groove inside the rim for a circular lid, a central drain-hole and a raised footring showing that it stood, not on a pedestal or shaft, but on paved ground (**85**). The whole subject of pre-Norman fonts in Britain is rather uncertain and many of those claimed to be earlier than the Conquest may be late eleventh century, but a slightly larger though otherwise very close match to the Tintagel font is that now at St Mary's, Potterne (Wiltshire). The Potterne font came from a Late Saxon timber church in the same village, where the late Dr Norman Davey's excavation – the site happened to be in his own garden – even pin-pointed the floor-level hollow within the church where this font had stood. The consensus is that it dates from the mid-tenth century. If, therefore, at Tintagel a first small stone church with a font is proposed at some date in the tenth century, the foundations

85 *Fragments of a tub font of volcanic greenstone, probably tenth century, from the foundations of the pre-Norman church, Tintagel churchyard. (Scale bar, 40 cm.) The original dimensions were: external diameters, rim 71 cm (28 in), base at footring 34 cm (13 in), height 38 cm (15 in) (photo: author.)*

exposed in 1991 may be those of a *second* church, in turn dismantled when the parish church was built in the early twelfth. Tentatively, this second church could be assigned to around AD 1000; and it is likely that its consecrated slate *mensa*, or altar-surface, is the one now preserved in the so-called Lady Chapel of the parish church (since it is rather different from the chamfered granite *mensa*, now missing, that would almost certainly have served as the Norman main altar-top).

It is the discovery of the remnants of this Period III, tenth-century font that raises important issues. Provision for baptism, and also in the churchyard provision for formal burial – here in the shape of an unusual gravetype, the walled grave (**86**) with its elongated oval outline and sides of low slate walling – imply in effect that the first (destroyed) church, and the second church represented by the foundation-course, served as 'parish churches' before the Conquest. At this point it is helpful to move some 8 km (5 miles) north-eastward up the coast, to the mother-church of Boscastle – Minster, or Talcarn.

Talcarn (Cornish *tal carn* '(place in) the brow of the rock') describes its situation, in a hollow at the top of a sheltered valley; Minster, unique in Cornwall as a parish name, its history. This was a pre-Conquest community, serving an area of at least six later parishes (Trevalga, Forrabury, Minster, St Juliot, Lesnewth and Otterham) surrounded by its own estate. The patroness was St Materiana or Mertheriana; the church held her shrine-tomb until the Reformation and the huge greenstone lid, probably pre-Conquest, survives unrecognized on the floor within. Minster's small off-centre chancel, sometimes called 'Early Norman', is in fact most of a late tenth- (or early eleventh-) century rectangular church, the same size as the postulated second church in Tintagel churchyard. Within the whole district, Minster represents the key ecclesiastical site of Period III and, as will be shown, is linked to Tintagel.

The Tintagel coastal belt at the time of Domesday (1086) was divided between two large holdings, *Botcinnii* (Bossiney) and *Tretdeno* (Treknow). Both were among the extensive lands of St Petroc's monastery at Bodmin, Treknow being in the monastery's hands and Bossiney having a tenant – *Eluui* or Alfwy, an Englishman. Where these manors met is not certain. Treknow certainly lay west of the Tintagel valley, south-west of the village, and as far as the next valley westward at Trebarwith or Port William. Bossiney stretched eastward, stopping short of Trevalga, whose small parish was a royal estate seized for King William. Tintagel Island and the site of the Castle were within Bossiney, as we know from Earl Richard's purchase in 1233–6. The parish church and churchyard of Tintagel were probably in Treknow. St Petroc's monastery at Bodmin was in the tenth century a major, and powerful, foundation, possessing the relics of the saint (a semi-legendary Period II figure, said to have come from south-west Wales) and owning numerous outlying lands. It is therefore at least possible that, in considering the origin of the supposedly two successive pre-Conquest churches partly uncovered in Tintagel churchyard, they should be regarded as Bodmin foundations; in which case, both are likely to have had St Petroc as patron. The early 'parochial' status indicated by a font, and associated formal burials, suggests that these lands were owned by St Petroc's monastery as early as 900–950, and that provision was being made for the tenants and peasants within an area of about 20 sq. km (8 sq. miles).

Why then, given this scenario, is there at Tintagel the subsequently-modified core of a

86 *Tintagel churchyard, 1991: a walled grave, of unusual construction.*

large cruciform church, dedicated in the name not of St Petroc but of St Materiana, and built some time after 1100 partly with walling-stone taken from a previous church? The answer was sketched, as an example of a 'discourse', in the first chapter (p. 20); it will have been the work of the Bottreaux family who, as lords of Boscastle, succeeded to the lay proprietorship of Minster. Some older relic of St Petroc may well have been preserved (and incorporated in a side-altar), but the new church was a Norman daughter-foundation of St Materiana of Minster.

The Island in Period III – the Chapel

There are various puzzles surrounding the small building of the Chapel. In the first instance, the records of the name of its supposed patron saint (mentioned earlier in Chapter 2 – see p. 28) show, as they do also in the contexts of St Juliot and of Lanteglos by Camelford, confusion between a 'Juliot' or 'Juliane' (an obscure male(?) Celtic figure) and the better-evidenced *Julitta* (St Julitta of Tarsus, usually linked with her son, Cyriacus or 'Cyres'). As it now stands – roofless, some of the walling replaced in the present century and known to have been partially excavated in the last (p. 28) – this Chapel has been presented as a structure of two phases. Radford's 1935 interim report summarized them. Its western end, a simple rectangle, was allegedly built in the middle of the twelfth century – this is to coincide with Earl Reginald's supposed creation of the Castle in 1141 and shortly afterwards. The second, enlargement, phase was dated to the thirteenth century, coinciding with Earl Richard's modification and completion of the Castle. In this, the Chapel was extended eastwards, provided with a little chancel step and side-grooves to take a chancel screen (**87**). A new doorway was fashioned on the south side, near the west end. Two stubby walls protruding from the west end formed a porch with inner benches, protecting an original west doorway. The dating of the first phase was confirmed not so much by the supposed link with Earl Reginald, Geoffrey of Monmouth and the earliest possible date of 1141, but by Romanesque or Norman ornament on some surviving carved stones. In the Celtic monastery model, the Chapel was patently far too late to have had any connection with a Christian community of the fifth to eighth centuries. The assumption was therefore that St Juliot or Julian(e) in the fifth century had been the founder of 'probably a simple church or oratory', which had vanished, and that the Chapel 'no doubt replaced the original monastic church'.

During the CAU's 1988 work on the Inner Ward, a full set of drawings of the Chapel had to be made in advance of repointing which has tended to obscure some of the masonry details. As a result, revisionism here has been brusque and total. What today's visitor sees is a small private extra-parochial church, a free chapel serving the Castle from 1233–6 until the fifteenth or early sixteenth century. It was probably well and richly furnished, and an endowed priest, who may or may not have had to reside in the Inner Ward, acted as chaplain. The internal burials noticed by Wilkinson (p. 29)

87 *The Chapel interior, east end, as now presented; note the rebuilt altar block with a plain granite slab, the low 'chancel' step and (in north wall, left) a groove cut to take a transverse screen. (photo: RCHME).*

may be those of such chaplains. The probability that this Period IV building had an earlier existence in Period III (i.e. before 1230) rests not on Radford's incorrect first phase but on the following considerations. First, the reported dedication to the obscure St Juliot is most unlikely to have anything to do with Earl Richard or a royal castle, and it tends to link the Chapel with one or more of the other places having this dedication. Second, the unusual position, which is extra-mural – right outside the Inner Ward, up some inconvenient steps – implies that this was already a Christian site before the 1230s. Third, though the various carved and worked stones known to have come from the Chapel can only be generally dated, as a group they are certainly not as late as the 1230s; an earlier horizon is obvious.

The archaeological answer was first given, and most persuasively, by the CAU team under Nic Appleton-Fox in their report. Though the whole sequence of superimposed foundations of whatever date – Period II, Period IV or anything else – in Radford's Site A cannot be disentangled now from the incomplete reports, Maclean's mid-nineteenth-century plan (see **19**) confirms that for some reason this was the only spot on the Island where a pattern of early walling had survived, visibly, and could be still indicated on a sketch; it probably explains why Site A was the first to be tackled in 1933. The basis of the Chapel is now seen to be a surviving rectangular room or building, possibly from the Post-Roman Period II, selected because it was unusually long (externally 13.5 by 5.3 m, or about 44 by 17½ ft – internally, it is 11.75 m by 3.7 m, or 38½ by 12 ft), and because its axis was approximately east–west – actually 11 degrees south of east. On the longer walls the breaks indicated by Radford as evidence for the removal of the twelfth-century eastern end when the Chapel was extended eastward in the 1230s are in fact traces of original north-side and south-side doorways. The surviving foundations were used to rebuild the walls; the south-side doorway was narrowed to provide a window and a new doorway made nearer the south-west corner. Secondary (Period IV, Castle) modifications included insertion of

88 *St Juliot's Chapel on the Island;*
reconstructed view from the south, as it may have
*looked in the thirteenth century (*Tracey Croft*).*

screen-grooves and low chancel step. The 'porch', in which there is no evidence at all for inner benches, is also secondary. It may have been intended to support a small upper room or store with access by a short ladder (**88**). It can also be pointed out that when in 1988 the worn grass within this porch was taken up, an apparent occupation-level with Period II imported pottery (B.i, B.iv and a Phocaean Red Slip rim) was exposed immediately below it.

The replaced granite slab, an unconsecrated altar surface on which an officiating priest could rest a portable, consecrated, super-altar has already been mentioned (p. 51). More puzzling is a small fine-granite font (**89**). This was removed from the Island, reportedly from the ruins of the Chapel, earlier this century; retained by a builder at nearby St Teath who had collection of such stones; and then presented to the parish church at Tintagel, where it is now kept. Another piece from the Chapel, a

triangular slab with a relief-carved marigold pattern rosette, can also been seen at the church built into a modern side-altar in the north transept (**90**). The font, only 33 cm (13 in) high and 56 cm (22 in) across, is probably the oldest item – late eleventh century? Given that the other fragments from the Chapel (including one, a side-slab with relief sunken star ornament sketched *in situ* by Thomas Hardy) may be very early twelfth century, 1100 can provisionally be suggested as a central date for the Period III conversion of a previous structure into a chapel. In fact the presence of the font means that it can more properly be described as an isolated church.

As a Period III phenomenon, this is still difficult to explain historically. Tintagel Island lay in the later manor of Bossiney. By 1166 Bossiney and other lands had passed to Reginald, Earl of Cornwall (so created in 1140) and Bossiney was held in demesne by a tenant, Roger de Mandeville. By 1182 the tenancy had been inherited by Gervase de Hornicote, whose grandson, also called Gervase, was to convey Tintagel to Earl Richard in May 1233. It is very hard to envisage circumstances in which a full

89 *Small fine-granite font, now in Tintagel church, from the Island Chapel. It is similar to three others in Cornwall, from Germoe, Sithney and Treslothan, all certainly eleventh-century and perhaps just before the Norman conquest* (photo: RCHME).

90 *A carved stone from the Island Chapel, now built into a side-altar, in the north transept of Tintagel church. Of twelfth-century style (the hexafoil rosette occurs on Cornish twelfth-century fonts, for example at Lewannick) this may be an internal gable-piece* (photo: RCHME).

parochial church of St Materiana for Tintagel having been built about 1120–40, any smaller but rival church – with rights of baptism if not of burial – could have appeared so nearby and in the same parish. If the Island Chapel is older – before 1120, conceivably even before 1086 but with some early twelfth-century embellishments – it might be explained as intended to serve *Botcinnii*, Bossiney, while the predecessor church at Tintagel served *Tretdenou*, Treknow; proximity allowing a single priest to minister at both. However, since both lands belonged to the monastery of St Petroc's it might be expected that the Island Chapel's ascription would be to *that* saint, rather than to St Juliot.

The second interpretation is for the moment preferable, and for another reason. There is independent evidence, in Period III, for the presence in the whole district of a wave of supposedly pious church-building thegns, squires or major tenants, with English names. Historically the most likely phase after which the Church, at any rate in north and east

Cornwall, was remodelled into the full Southern English proto-parochial minster system would be following the reign of Aethelstan (924–39). Descendants of incoming ninth-century English landowners would have intermarried with the native Cornish; maintenance of the cults of purely Cornish saints can be expected. If Domesday Book is used as a partial guide at 1086, late in a century that probably saw a fair amount of church-building, before 1066 St Juliot had been held by Edwy, *Tregrebri* (? Genver, just east of Tintagel) by the same or another Edwy, the lands of Talcarn or Minster by Edwin, and the paramount holding of *Henliston* (Helstone in Trigg, including St Juliot's other church at Lanteglos) by Algar. These are all English or Anglo-Scandinavian names. People from this group figure on contemporary, still visible, Period III monuments.

The eleventh-century cross-slab now outside the Wharncliffe Arms hotel in Tintagel shows on one face the names of the four Evangelists, MATHEUS . MARCUS . LUCAS . IOHA(nes), their bearded faces in the angles of an expanded-arm cross (**91**). The other side has AELRIAT (or less probably AELNAT) FECIT HA(n)C CRUCEM P(ro) ANIMA SUA, 'A. made this cross for the sake of

91 *Tintagel; mutilated stone cross 1.3 m (4¼ ft) high, now outside the Wharncliffe Arms Hotel, rescued from nearby Trevillet where it was used as a gatepost.* (Drawing: A.G. Langdon, 1890.)

his soul'. It could well have been erected by a man building an estate church at Trevalga, replaced there after 1100 by the present parish church. Outside Lanteglos church is a tall narrow slab of granite, the summit socketed for a missing cross-head, and inscribed vertically in rather an archaic fashion down the face and down one side. We read that Aelselth and Genereth wrought this *sybstel* (monument: literally, 'family-pillar') for Aelwine's soul and for themselves. Aelwine was presumably Aelselth's father and Genereth (a Cornish name?) his wife. The stone came from Castle Goff half a mile west, where there is an undated small earthwork, and dates to about AD 1000, or a little later. There is also a broken cross-shaft with remains of a late interlace ornament standing at Waterpit Down 6 km (4 miles) east of Tintagel by the old road eastward to Launceston; it is either late tenth or early eleventh century and a basal panel has the lettering CR/UX/ME/VR/OC – *crux mevroc* – 'The Cross of Meuroc, or Meurog' (probably a Cornish name, that of the pious benefactor who commissioned it as a guide-mark).

In the context of this evidence, which is interesting enough on its own (only the highlights are given here), it could be suggested

that the Island Chapel was originally a privately-built estate church for Bossiney, a Period III pre-Conquest venture, converted in the first half of the eleventh century from a handy Period II ruin. The dedication to St Juliot – if John Leland's testimony is accepted – may have been inspired by contemporary church-building at one or other of the nearby St Juliot church-sites. It is possible that the place was slightly improved with carved ornamented work in the early twelfth century, but it seems even more likely that, from before the middle of that century, it was eclipsed by Tintagel parish church and may have fallen into disuse. Any such fate did not prevent a subsequent employment, with structural modifications, after 1233 as an extra-parochial endowed chapel serving the Castle.

The considerable quantity of medieval pottery from the Island is almost all of the thirteenth century or later, and represents the domestic equipment of the Castle's builders and subsequent occupants. There are however a few fragments (from 1933–8, and unhappily not provenanced) of a distinctive Somerset chert-tempered ware, cooking-pots that are twelfth century and not thirteenth. They may indicate a party of masons, or an occasionally-resident priest (in another rebuilt Period II room on Site A?) in and around the Chapel after 1100 and in this connection the implication of the incised pictorial slates should be considered. Medium-sized or big pieces of local slate with suitable flat faces were used for quick designs or careful drawings, scratched with a knife-point. Chronologically these are quite distinct from the primary cross-marked stones found at the churchyard. They date to late in Period III or early in Period IV and it is very doubtful if any is as old as Period II. Those from the Island are not at all well provenanced. A certain amount of nonsense has been written about them in the past, but they have now been properly published with fully accurate drawings by Carl Thorpe. Some of these slates (Period IV) show designs for board games – 'Merrells' or Nine Men's Morris, or the simpler 'Achi' – of the fox-and-geese kind played with two colours of pebbles (**92**). Others are a little more complicated.

Those from the parish churchyard include both games, and general doodling and sketching, done by masons engaged to build the church from about 1120 onward. The interest-

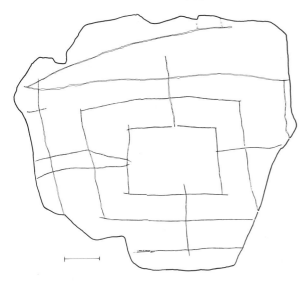
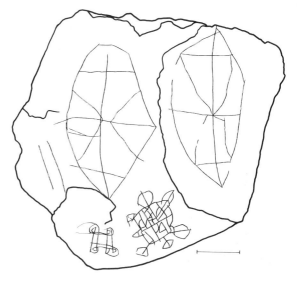

92 *Samples, from about a dozen slates found so far at Tintagel Island and churchyard, of roughly incised surfaces for board-games (twelfth–fourteenth centuries). (Left) Island (IS.2, unprovenanced) – for merrells or Nine Men's Morris. (Right) Churchyard (1991), for games of the Achi kind. (Scale bars, 6 cm; drawn by Carl Thorpe.)*

ing discovery is that one particular slate (IS 7) – which *is* known to have been found in the 1930s over a pit by the north wall of the Island chapel – may have been scratched by the same hand as another slate, found in 1991 at the churchyard. The Island piece has two very odd depictions of armed men with pointed helmets, a sword, and circular rather than heater-shaped shields (they are, if anything, as much Late Saxon as Norman) and two versions of a design of a cross involving looped chequerboard lines curled out at the four corners. The same design, simple and complex, is repeated on a churchyard slate that also has the layout for a game and an extraordinary little creature, a vivid thumbnail sketch of a Common Logger-head turtle (**93**). These animals, natives of the American coast, are frequently stranded on Cornish shores; the Tintagel turtle, perhaps an unfortunate washed up in the Haven in the twelfth century, is the earliest such representation in European art by many centuries. Another piece, or rather two joining pieces (IS 5, IS 6), were 'picked up among the stones fallen from the medieval chapel' (so Radford in his 1935 report) 'where they had been reused as building material'. They form a panel with an expanded-arm cross incised within a border, the original being about 30 cm (12 in) across; the absence of any name tends to rule out a headstone for a grave, and this may be a small frontal-panel for the altar block of the original, eleventh-century, chapel or estate church (**94**).

Oddly, for a complex of sites associated from time to time with important people and the outside world, virtually no coins come from Tintagel (apart from the small Late Roman hoard, p. 84). A cluster, of shillings down to halfpennies, William II to Victoria, was recovered from the 1930s work, reflecting touristic carelessness. No credence can be placed in two finds: a bronze coin of Magnentius (AD 354–61), said to have been found 'in a well near Tintagel Castle', and a silver penny of Alfred the Great, a type late in his reign (871–99), allegedly picked up near the Chapel. In 1991 a silver penny of Henry II (1154–89) was found in the churchyard, interestingly within a rubble spread associated with the demolition of the small church preceding the construction of the present parish church; it accords with the architectural opinion that the original cruciform structure of about 1120–40 was further modified throughout the twelfth century.

Bossiney Mound
Finally, within Period III, there is Bossiney Mound. Though the casual visitor today could be forgiven for regarding Tintagel village and

93 *(Left) Graffiti on a slate from the Island (IS7), found over a pit by the north wall of the Chapel in the 1930s. (Right, below) Similar 'checker-and-loops' motifs from a Churchyard slate, 1991. (Above) An enlargement of the Turtle (see **92**) – beaked head at top, stumpy tail at bottom, extra flipper. (Scale bar 6 cm; drawn by Carl Thorpe.)*

Bossiney (on the road out to Boscastle) as simply the two ends of a ribbon development, Bossiney and Tintagel are quite distinct settlements with distinctive histories, as the historian of Bossiney rightly reminds us. Bossiney Mound, incongruously next to the Methodist Chapel, is a small earthen ringwork or castle. It may have been built at some time after the Conquest by the de Mandevilles. When Tintagel Castle was built in the 1230s, there would have been no point in maintaining it; and archaeologically, though never excavated, it forms a prime site because anything found there will date from about the end of the eleventh century to the decade 1230–40. There are a number of these small Norman earthwork castles, ring-works or motte-and-bailey type, in north-east Cornwall – the establish-

ment of the Bottreaux family at Boscastle may have been the largest – and very little is known about them.

Castle, Church and District – Period IV

As medieval castles go, Tintagel Castle is neither very elaborate nor of any particular interest. Apart from its dramatic siting and its connection with Richard, Earl of Cornwall, there is little to recommend it. Okehampton Castle, outside the town on a rocky spur in the valley of the West Ockment, is actually just as picturesque, better preserved, fully explored, larger and with a detailed history stretching from the eleventh to the fifteenth century. In Cornwall itself the castles at Launceston and Restormel remain the real targets for castle-lovers.

The known history of Earl Richard's castle can be summarized briefly because there is not much to write. Richard lived until 1272; his youthful concern with Cornwall's legendary past was set aside for larger goals. As far as is known, nobody ever attacked or defended Tintagel. Richard was accused of giving shelter there to his nephew David, a rebellious Welsh prince of Gwynedd, in 1245; it is not certain

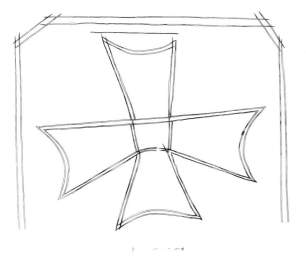

94 *A slate plaque from the Chapel, Tintagel Island, with an incised outline cross and bordure; precise date and function uncertain. The reconstruction drawing is made from two large joining fragments (by the author). (Scale bar, 6 cm.)*

that this really took place. Conceivably, Richard made a flying visit in 1256, when he was spending Christmas at his larger and more convenient seat of Launceston Castle; if so, no other Earl or Duke of Cornwall is recorded as having visited Tintagel until October 1987, when the present Duke spend a happy afternoon exploring the Island. In 1328 the young prince, John of Eltham, brother of King Edward III, became Earl of Cornwall. Tintagel Castle since 1272, the year of Richard's death, had been in the care of successive Sheriffs of Cornwall and in 1305 one of them (Thomas de la Hyde) kept accounts showing the Castle staffed by a Constable, a resident chaplain and a few minor functionaries. Repairs of a routine nature were being carried out.

During John of Eltham's short earldom, however, the timber principals from the roof of the Great Hall (which would have been valuable as well as long) were taken down and stored somewhere on the site. John died in 1336, aged 20; Edward III then created his first-born son Edward, aged six, the next earl. Prince Edward of Woodstock is better known as the Black Prince. Inheritor of the considerable Earldom (and from 1337, Duchy) estates, he attempted a partial restoration of his castle at Tintagel. The Captain of Seisin, a 1337 survey of all the Duchy properties, describes conditions there. Not all of it is familiar. There is mention of two chambers over the gateway, a long-vanished upper element above the Lower Ward entrance presumably communicating sideways with the Upper Ward. There was a chamber with a small kitchen for the Constable – this would be a fourteenth-century modification within the site of the Great Hall – a stable for eight horses (in the Lower Ward), a cellar and a disused bakehouse. The removal of the Hall's roof-beams 'because the said Hall was ruinous and the walls of no strength' is specified. Reference to the Chapel with its resident priest daily celebrating the Divine Office, and to the Constable, show us the bare complement of these two officials. The cellar (*celarium*) may be the Tunnel, beyond Site D (p. 48), and the ruined bakehouse (*pistrina*) one of the rooms or buildings at Site D with its domed stone oven. Interestingly, as far back as 1337 there is a note that the rough grazing on the Island, *pastura infra castrum* 'the grazing beyond the Castle', was worth two shillings a year and presumably leased out.

The Black Prince was in Cornwall in 1354, and again in 1363, at Restormel Castle. Possibly Tintagel and other Cornish castles were given a token restoration on the first, or both, of these occasions. After 1337 the history of the Castle emerges, faintly, from occasional mentions. These, and the findings of the 1988 survey work, have yet to be collated and explored; the present book is not a suitable place in which to devote pages to any detailed synopsis, within which visible architectural features may or may not match such fragmentary records. During the Black Prince's time, the Great Hall was probably reconstructed on a smaller scale, the offices – such as a kitchen and buttery – in the space north-west of the Hall being modified. In the fourteenth century a two-storeyed dwelling – living quarters – was built within the Great Hall's ground-area (**95**). From time to time, because the place was suitably remote, State prisoners were despatched to Tintagel in the custody of the resident Constable. John de Northampton, Lord Mayor of London, was allegedly there in 1385; Thomas, Earl of Warwick, certainly so in 1307. Dr Radford has identified various features added in the later fourteenth century: the additional cross-wall behind the Iron Gate's main

95 *Remains of two-storeyed, fourteenth-century lodging, built inside the shell of the Great Hall, seen from the west. Only the longer foundation, next to and parallel with the footpath, can be accepted as a genuine modern consolidation (of the west long-side of the Hall)* (photo: RCHME).

thirteenth-century fortification, a separate two-roomed structure within the Inner Ward across the path opposite the Great Hall.

Later mentions in topographical literature have already been cited in earlier chapters, discussing such topics as the elusive draw-bridge (p. 37). They also chronicle the place's progressive decay. In 1478 William Worcestre was informed that Tintagel Castle was *dirutum fortissimum*, 'Very strong, but in ruins'. John Leland in about 1540 saw how 'the residew of the buildings of the castel be sore wether beten and in ruine (but it hath been a large thinge)'. Leland, a prototype country gentleman as well as an antiquary, had a keen eye for what nowadays would be called The Environment.

He observed that there were sheep on Tintagel Island (the first such record) and they grazed on ground that 'now nuryshyth shepe and conys'. The 'conys' or conies were rabbits, introduced in Norman times for food. A few years earlier (1537) there had been a proposal to lease the site of the Castle with the Island for the grazing of rabbits therein, at what was said to be 'an ancient rent' for it: 6s 8d, or a third of a pound.

Returning now to the early thirteenth century, and supposing that with the agreement of the de Hornicote family the young Earl Richard had personally visited the Island in 1230, gone there again with a surveyor of works or master-mason and planned out the sort of mock-Arthurian castle he wanted, and in 1233 with a signed agreement had begun to construct this in earnest, all sorts of things follow. An enormous quantity of building-slate had to be quarried (most of it, certainly, from exposed rock-faces on the Island, some still detectable) and trimmed for use. Greenstone, for coigns and detailing, had to be hacked out from the basal courses of the Island or from the Barras

Nose spur in the Haven, and dressed on site. The whole place, except for the isolated Chapel deserted since the end of Period III, would require a good deal of ground-level preparation. Cost was not a material obstacle. Assuming that something like fifty men – labourers, masons, specialists – would have to be housed, fed and serviced on site, and this for a couple of years at the minimum, where was this happy band to be accommodated? Not in a village that, almost certainly, did not yet exist. The idea that most if not all of the longer rectangular stone-walled huts, on the southern and eastern sides of the Island, were the temporary homes for the Castle work-force in summer and winter alike therefore has a realistic backing. Cathy O'Mahoney, in her 1988 examination of all the medieval pottery, found that the whole collection consisted of 1105 sherds, representing 408 different vessels, most of them thirteenth and fourteenth century. Only 165 of the sherds were marked and thus provenanced, a marked defect of the 1930s work; the pots thus cannot be linked to specific sites, though at least 34 came from Site A.

The dominating impression is that, in the process of planning the Castle's layout, the ground-plan was almost entirely influenced by what had happened in Period II. To this extent the youthful Earl Richard was indeed treading in the footsteps of bygone kings. The Great Ditch had been dug to produce a narrow entry in the lee of the natural crag housing the landward-side Upper Ward; therefore this had to become the Period IV gateway, just as the outer wall of the Lower Ward had to be footed along the line of the Period II rampart. The Iron Gate's defended landing-point, with its path going up to the Inner Ward, merely revived the Period II natural wharf and access. On the Island, the optimum point for high-status use was the natural hollow on its south-east corner, facing the mainland; here, the Inner Ward and the Great Hall would obviously have to be placed.

The minor excavations of 1988 filled in what had been a large gap in the Castle's story. In 1230 Richard probably saw an irregularly sloping hollow, surrounded by rocky outcrops with traces of two or three much-overgrown terraces, fitting into the hillside at the corner of the Island, and approached immediately across the saddle or neck. In order to make a levelled surface for his Great Hall, the first long retaining-wall or curtain-wall had to be built. Its inner base was double-thickness, for stability, though instead of being rooted in the bedrock it was actually set in a compacted stratum of soil with stones and occupation debris. This curtain wall, up to 3 m (10 ft) high in places, was well made, its outer face being staged or stepped, and the northern end of the original stretch was finished with dressed greenstone blocks (**96**). Using it as a kind of dam, a huge mass of loose soil, broken slates, more occupation debris with pottery, bone, ash and assorted Period II rubbish, and hacked-up turf was flung or shovelled into the retained space, eventually providing a fairly large artificial platform.

On this surface the 1233 Hall was built, a double-square in plan. Allowing for the thickness of the walls it may have been pegged out

96 *Outer (east) wall of the Inner Ward; junction between the first curtain-wall, with ashlar corner, below the Great Hall (left) and the additional curtain-wall (right) (photo: Susanna Thomas).*

97 *Buttress, added in the 1240s(?) to support the 1233–6 curtain-wall below the Great Hall; the pole (true vertical) shows how the inner face of the buttress conforms to the outward bulge of the curtain-wall* (photo: Susanna Thomas).

as (in modern feet) 32 by 64 or roughly 10 by 20 m. But the sheer weight of these thick slate walls, and the lateral pressure exerted by the mass of material (made both heavier and more mobile as surface-water percolated), caused the retaining curtain-wall to start bulging outwards. One might well guess that, within a decade, this became a matter of serious concern. Around 1240, then, the master-mason of the day was obliged to plan remedial action. Not the least of the pleasures of an archaeologist's life are those rare occasions when one can be absolutely confident, when inspecting the distant past, what happened next. In this case, firm activity followed. Four stout buttresses, spaced I – II – I, were built against the outside of the curtain-wall to control the lateral movement; their inner faces are, as it were, 1240-period photographs recording permanently the precise shape of the dangerous out-

ward bulge (**97**). Probably at the same time, with a labour-force at hand (and archaeologically this means renewed occupation, more cooking-pots and beer-jugs, more beef-bones and general rubbish), a secondary curtain-wall was added, curving around northward to retain another smaller area of filled and levelled ground on which separate service rooms, beyond the Great Hall, could be raised. A couple more buttresses were for safety's sake added to this new curtain; here, their upper parts are bonded across into the high outer wall that formed the seaward side of the new service wing. All of this is fully visible; it can all be read like a large-print book; the wonder is that it was not so read in the past (**98**).

The evidence of the 1988 'Soakaway' cutting provided the missing pieces in this puzzle. There is hardly any record of the 1930s small trenches – 'Site Z' – made against the outer base of the curtain-wall, except that stones set in clay and a fair quantity of Period II finds were encountered up to two feet below the grass. Even before it had been filled back, it was possible to draw a profile (**99**) involving both Site Z and the Soakaway cutting, suggesting that walling, finds, and thus an occupation-level of post-Roman character stretched from one to the other, underlying the thirteenth-century fill below the Great Hall. Rather later, it was noticed that if viewed through field-glasses at the end of the Lower Ward above the present steep steps down to the neck, the section visible in the opposite cliff-face – below the ruinous southern end of the Great Hall – confirms such a profile (**100**). It also shows that the first curtain-wall, the lower part of which here has a lower and separate inner element, is (extraordinarily) not footed in bedrock at all but appears to have been constructed in a trench dug down into compacted occupation.

Without a major excavation (technically feasible but at the present time prohibitively expensive) we cannot be sure what form the post-Roman occupation in this hollow below the Inner Ward assumed. That it was probably terraced is implied by the location, the use of terracing elsewhere on the Island and apparently also by the cliff-section. Some of what was there has been lost. The southern end of the Great Hall, some 3 or 4 m (10 or 13 ft) of it along with the southernmost of the four external buttresses, fell away into the chasm in the last century. Occupation rubbish, dominated by

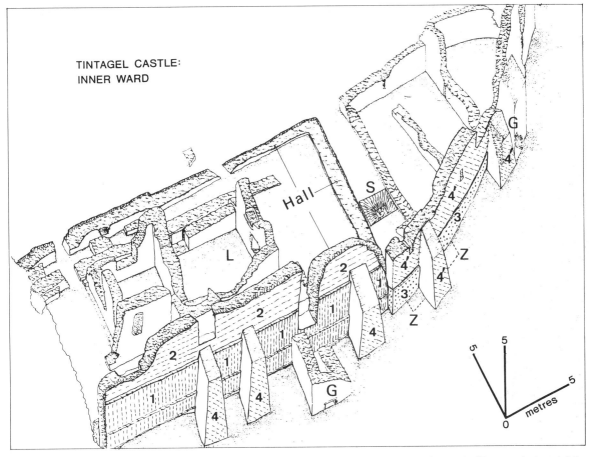

TINTAGEL CASTLE: INNER WARD

98 *The Inner Ward: isometric drawing from the east (CAU 1988). Sequence: 1, first retaining curtain-wall (1230/1236), with 2, wall of the Great Hall built upon a retained platform. 3 Additional or secondary curtain-wall (1240 + ?) to enclose service-end. 4 Main buttresses – one now lost over the cliff – to support first curtain-wall (1240s), with 4', raising of wall no.3 with two bonded buttresses. G Later garderobe chutes. S the CAU's 1986 'Soakaway' cutting. Z Approximate positions of Radford's 1930s cuttings at the outer base of wall. L Two-storeyed lodging (fourteenth-century) built inside the shell of the Great Hall.*

imported pottery, may have spilled down the slope towards the Haven; this is the context of William Taylor's 1918 'Cliff Fall' finds (p. 30). But below the Great Hall should be the postulated royal lodgings of post-Roman times. By medieval, let alone modern, standards such quarters may have been cramped and grubby.

As far as all the evidence indicates, it is within this hollow, underlying at least half of the Inner Ward, that the remains should be sought.

Elsewhere on the Island, Period IV features like the Tunnel and the various watering-points have already been described (Chapter 3). As for the Chapel, when brought into the service of the Castle its post-1230 function was to serve as a chantry, endowed by the Earldom and subsequently the Duchy, where a maintained priest could daily pray for the repose of the souls of Richard, Earl of Cornwall and King of the Germans, and his successors in the title. Lastly, what might be catalogued as the inner defences must be discussed (**101**). Climbing the recut stone steps and entering the Inner Ward today, the curving wall with its arched doorway and the odd little 'love-seat' just inside are all R.B. Kinsman's 1852 improvements. The high wall, with the remains of another doorway, separating the Inner Ward from the rest of the Island, is Period IV. The castellations on the top of the wall are not Kinsman's additions, as

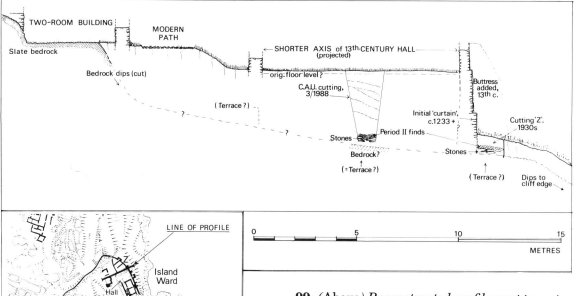

99 *(Above) Reconstructed profile west to east (line indicated on the inset plan) just north of the Great Hall – side-walls of the Hall and the line of the first retaining curtain-wall projected northward into the profile. Remains of clay-set stone walling and post-Roman finds from the base of the CAU's 1988 cutting ('Soakaway') and Radford's 1930s Site Z cutting belong to the same episode/occupation/date.*

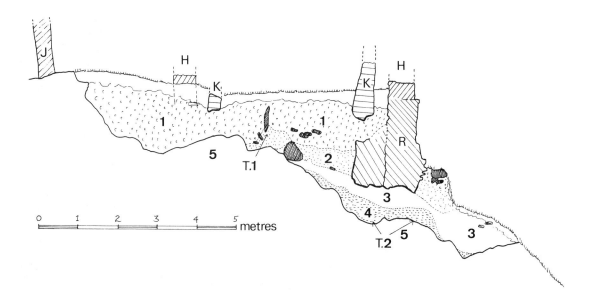

101 *Northern defensive wall of the Inner Ward with the gateway opening to the rest of the Island; a view of 1895–1900 in the post-Kinsman, pre-Office of Works era and before any twentieth-century reconstruction (*photo: Gibson, Penzance*).*

so often wrongly cited. They appear, clearly, in views from the 1820s. It is arguable that all this inner wall is secondary but, if so, probably added in the 1240s when the buttresses were built. It is in fact a witness to a thirteenth-

100 *(Left) Section, west to east, across the south end of the Inner Ward exposed in the cliff-face (drawn from photographs and through binoculars by Carl Thorpe). J End of Kinsman's 1852 wall by entrance. K End-walls of fourteenth-century lodging. H Ends of longer-side walls of the Great Hall. R End of the first retaining curtain-wall (doubled at base). Layers: 1 Main fill, soil and stones; 2 darker grey layer; 3 reddish-brown layer, perhaps remnant of Period II occupation, with large pot-sherds visible through binoculars; 4 medium greyish-brown, possibly buried soil; and 5 bedrock slate. T.1, T.2, are the most likely lines of any Period II built terraces.*

century recognition that the Inner Ward might be attacked following an unopposed landing at the Iron Gate rocks.

As seen today by the visitor, the Inner Ward seems a confusing jumble and no analytical interpretation is offered. The whole ward has never been systematically explored; on the steep slope above the two-roomed building, still within the natural hollow and the remains of the thirteenth-century surrounding wall, there may well be traces of Period II use. A secondary phase of the Great Hall was detected in the course of the 1988 survey, involving the construction of a garderobe chute (a primitive lavatory) against the outer face separate from the buttresses, and perhaps internal divisions. The question of any upper (first-floor) rooms, known as 'solars', above any part of the Hall or the service-rooms, is a difficult one. Discovery of a narrow keystone-like block, perhaps the central heading of an arched doorway or window, with a low relief cross on it (**102**) raises the chance that this is not some stray component from the Chapel but indicates use of an upper room as a private oratory. The ruined building (with stone staircase) inside the area of the Great Hall itself has two phases; the second and final phase saw a two-storey rectangular building, each floor with two rooms. In

102 *Architectural fragments with low-relief crosses, said to be from the Inner Ward; photographed when in store at Tintagel (1988). (Scale (matchbox) is 8 cm;* photo: author.*)*

the fourteenth century it must have been where a Constable (if ever genuinely resident) lodged, or where State prisoners were accommodated.

Turning to the matter of the presentation of the Inner Ward as an ancient monument in care, it is known from photographic evidence starting in the 1890s that there has been any amount of 'silent' reconstruction. This covers the display of ground-plan walling, only one or two courses deep, for which no justification can be found, and the pointing-up of wall junctions that simply did not exist in that guise. The accusing finger points not at Constable R.B. Kinsman but at the staff of the former Office of Works.

The account of the Castle in Period IV provided in this chapter has been intentionally little more than a sketch, dwelling on individual features of interest. The mainland Lower and Upper Wards have not been discussed at any length because there is little, supportable by hard evidence, that could be written about them. The walls, or supposed rooms or cells, now on show in the Upper Ward constitute a hopeless jumble. Do they represent a guard-room, or a store, or what else? What is the evidence for date? Where exactly are the signs of any physical link to any rooms over the main Lower Ward gatehouse? Supersonic fighter aircraft based at Chivenor in north Devon were recently exercising up and down this coastline (as they have done for years). Two of them howled past, prohibitively low; their shock-wave brought down a considerable stretch of the Upper Ward's thirteenth-century surrounding wall on the seaward (western) side. This has been tidied up by the masons, but it is a sharp little reminder – and in a geophysical region where minor offshore earth-tremors often take place – that Tintagel Castle's remains diminish as time goes by. The archaeology of post-Roman times has so far proved the greater attraction to the archaeologists, but the definitive account of the medieval Castle, remarkable enough in its own right, has yet to be written. It may be some while before this responsibility is shouldered.

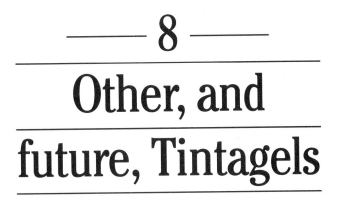

8

Other, and future, Tintagels

To generations of the Cornish, and to a greater number of people who visit Cornwall regularly, Tintagel has always possessed qualities beyond those of simple historical and archaeological interest. One might dismiss the impact as no more than impressions of the coastal scenery – the sun and the sky, the far-flung views with Lundy like a ghostly whale on the northern horizon, the realm of wild Nature and the intrusive presence of the sea (**103**). Admittedly these impressions are crucial, as with other ancient sites; imagine Stonehenge, relocated in the parking lot of a supermarket. It has been said of Stonehenge that there is not and never

103 *The Island, in rough weather, from Glebe Cliff; how long before the seas create a real Island here?* (Photo: RCHME.)

has been one, single, monument, but a different Stonehenge for every man, woman and child that sees it. This may also be true for Tintagel, as it is for Venice (and may well be for Euro-Disneyland). If so, it was true in the remote past. There are any number of 'other Tintagels', one at least for each aspect of the place as a monument.

Starting with the archaeology, a fair-minded archaeologist would have to admit that the record has been swamped by the picturesque but visually obtrusive Castle, and by the inordinate amount of Period II finds, thousands of them. We do not *know* that the place is really devoid of any prehistoric record; we assume that traces of any genuine, pre-Roman, occupation would by now have turned up at some point in all the nineteenth- and twentieth-century diggings, and they have not. We do not

104 *The memorial pillar at Castle Dore near Fowey, Cornwall 2.75 m (9 ft) high; a Christian tombstone of the early sixth century. The inscription, with some reversed and ligatured letters, reads DRUSTANUS ('Tristan') HIC IACIT CUNOMORI FILIUS, 'Drustanus lies here, son of Cunomorus'.*

know, either, what went on there during the Roman period; there is just enough to allow the idea of a 'Period I', but none of the material is specific enough to lead to anything better than guess work.

Similarly, for the historian or the student of literature nine and a half centuries of Arthurian noise have almost, though not completely, drowned a faint music from earlier days. It cannot be demonstrated beyond doubt that, before Geoffrey of Monmouth took up his pen, nobody had ever told tales that linked the British hero Arthur with Tintagel. There are, after all, echoes of Arthurian legends elsewhere in Cornwall (as there are in Wales, and Scotland, and several English regions). In the year 1113 (within our Period III) some canons of Laon in northern France were touring southwest England, raising funds to rebuild their

burnt-down cathedral. On Bodmin Moor, or perhaps Dartmoor, they were shown King Arthur's Chair and Oven among rock-formations, and at Bodmin there was a quarrel with the locals about whether or not King Arthur was still alive, in some secret refuge. Indeed Bodmin Moor still contains various 'Arthur' features. But was Geoffrey of Monmouth, like Walter Scott, merely adept at relocating likely chaps on likely maps?

What makes a Tintagel link, before Geoffrey's day, implausible is not so much the negative or missing evidence but the indication that stories from an entirely different cycle existed. To read Beroul's twelfth-century verse drama *Tristran* – either the hard way in his jerky Norman-French lines, or in any of the decent modern French or English translations – can be an unnerving experience, like entering a long-locked chamber, untouched for centuries. The poet himself is a shadow. He may have been a Frenchified Breton rather than a true Norman, but it is virtually sure that Beroul once wandered around Cornwall and that he wrote with an eye on patronage from the powerful Cardinham family living near Bodmin. In the sole manuscript of *Tristran*, the opening is lost and must be reconstructed from another, more polished, version by Gottfried von Strassburg. This is a pity but not a tragedy. We still have Beroul's *Tintajol*, *Tintaguel*, a stronghold and residence of King Mark, which is nowhere except the Island. How many ancient monuments are linked to a medieval text of this quality? There have been – there still are – many claimants to the original setting of Tristan and Iseult, but it can be stated that the male name *Drustanus* ('Tristan') occurs in a sixth-century Cornish memorial inscription (**104**) and the female name *Eselt* (as *hryt eselt*, 'Iseult's Ford') in a west Cornwall charter boundary of 967. These remain the oldest recorded, as opposed to inferred, instances of the names. As W.J. McCann reminds us, like many other originally independent heroes of Insular stories, Tristan was drawn into the Arthurian orbit – in Wales, perhaps as early as the eleventh century. But we may properly enquire: where did Beroul find the core of his own poetic version of the Tristan, Iseult and Mark story, if not in Cornwall? What was he told about Tintagel?

Ever since Geoffrey's *Historia*, and since Alfred Lord Tennyson at a galloping pace,

Arthurian Tintagel must share in a wider responsibility for a divergence between the Past As Wished For, and the Past As It May Really Have Been. Nowhere is the gap more pronounced than in respect of places, like the Island and the Castle, that really exist, and here a finger points sternly at Tintagel. Other locales like 'Camelot' remain shadowy, and also unidentified because most of them were never real and identifiable places. John Boorman's too long, but still enthralling, film *Excalibur* (1980) opens with a totally convincing reconstruction of an idealized, Period II, Celtic stronghold – his own version of Tintagel Island, mocked-up for the occasion on some lonely headland in Ireland. Boorman at least struck out by featuring a youthful Arthur and a young middle-aged Merlin. Different icons have long been frozen solid, exhibited in every form of visual art. Arthur, in most Pre-Raphaelite oils, in Hatherell's Tintagel paintings (p. 129) and in the 'King Arthur Pop-Up Books' which are now collectors' items, usually resembles a pensive and kindly model of the late King George V in a purple bathrobe, pointed slippers and spiky golden crown. The public is not interested in other forms of reality supported by academic research. There is no mileage in suggesting that a typical monarch in sixth-century Britain or Ireland would have been a short, wary-looking young man with bad teeth, bad breath, body lice and a suspicious temper. There is probably very little mileage, too, in a notion that Earl Richard's Castle never had a drawbridge (p. 37), or battlements where Agincourt-style banners fluttered in the breeze.

The mystic and ethereal perceptions of several sorts of Other Tintagels are of recent date. They either depart completely from the fragmentary Tristan, or Arthurian, texts, or else revert to the late Victorian folklorists who first pitched on the 'Arthur' of medieval literature as a symbol for a prehistoric sun-god (or the like). It could even be said, unkindly, that a fiction is giving birth to further little fictions. The writer finds himself in a quandary when it comes to noticing books about Tintagel that discuss the place, and its visible monuments, as a focus of enigmatic power through countless ages. Access to inner vision is undeniably anyone's right. In his latter years Thomas Hardy's inner vision (prosaic in comparison with others now circulating) led to *The Famous Tragedy of*

105 *Thomas Hardy's vision of Tintagel as the seat of King Mark; drawn from memory, 1923, as the frontispiece of his* The Famous Tragedy of the Queen of Cornwall.

the Queen of Cornwall, At Tintagel in Lyonnesse (Macmillan, 1923). The old man's verse drama is striking enough, but hard even to read aloud, and today it would be quite unperformable (**105**). Historians, doing their best to produce straightforward accounts about people and events at Tintagel across the centuries, try to take care not to confuse permissible inference with unsupported guesswork. They thus tend to be repelled by New Age writings that make no such distinction, appeal to 'facts' that cannot be shown to exist, and in short make use of historical and archaeological evidence without the necessary training in understanding either form. For instance, deductions from a totally hypothetical prehistoric landscape, said to surround Tintagel, do not acquire any force when the authority for them turns out to be an account of Neolithic and Bronze Age stone monuments on nearby Bodmin Moor, the construction of which is linked to the Sumerians. In such works the triumphantly-presented conclusions that rest on odd words and names snatched, like cherries on a cake, from all or any of the Celtic languages, only tell us that the authors are up a linguistic creek with no paddles, sinking rapidly.

The would-be reader might be directed to just two books. *The Mystery of Arthur at Tintagel* (1990) is written with fluency. All the archaeology, and almost all the Celtic language references, are just plain wrong, and therefore the author's constructs from what he takes to be factual data have no meaning. Why on earth should the medieval Tunnel (p. 46) give rise to the idea that its upper and lower entrances have a 'male' and 'female' feeling? If genuine, are such attributes common at other functional tunnels like a motorway underpass? The book's genesis is the 1924 Tintagel visit by the founder of Anthroposophy, the Austrian esoteric thinker Rudolf Steiner. But this and other, necessarily woolly, Tintagel-based outpourings are being shunted offstage by the prolific output from what many archaeologists (though not of course its practitioners) call 'Alternative Archaeology'. Here, as with instances of menhirs and stone circles, we encounter a chicken-and-egg dilemma. Which came first? Was Tintagel chosen as a citadel, a focus for legends, a medieval castle, *because* lines of energy and force are said to converge there; or are such postulated convergences the *result* of the choice of the site by forgotten priests and shamans? It is no bad thing, however, when the divining-rod – which can do no harm – takes over from the spade and gives a little respite to over-dug ancient monuments. Paul Broadhurst's *Tintagel and the Arthurian Mythos* (1992) is based on detailed research and illustrated with rare sympathy. For many readers it may call for too many suspensions of disbelief; that forms one of several good reasons to mention it here. It would be a grey world if ever the Thought Police outlawed all but academically-approved writings about a past we never knew, a country where none but the unnamed dead may dwell.

What all the mystics and New Age thinkers have, surprisingly, failed to notice is the peculiar *absence* of Otherworld legends attached to Tintagel, a place where one would justifiably expect to find them. On the Island at night there are no ghosts, no spectral beings, and usually nothing at all except for the independently-minded ginger cat who acts as resident caretaker and, following visits from mainland toms, occasionally produces kittens. The only known instance, which is a case of the widespread 'Disappearing Island' motif, concerns an alleged former belief that twice a year, at midsummer and again at midwinter, the whole Island temporarily vanishes. The Truro schoolmaster Thomas Hogg, a Scot born at Kelso in 1777, produced in 1827 his *The Fabulous History of the ancient Kingdom of Cornwall*. Apparently it was intended – but, annoyingly for Hogg, generally not so perceived

– as a satire on the learned and fanciful historians of Cornwall like Dr William Borlase. Of the Island, Hogg wrote:

> The wonderous fabric, twice a-year,
> From nature's face would disappear.
> At Christmas-eve, when blazing fires
> Illumed the halls with wreathing spires,
> Dissolved in clouds, it passed away,
> Like mist before the morning ray.
> When vernal flowers perfumed the plain.
> The pile, majestic, towered again.
>   When vaulted rose the summer skies,
> Again, it fled from mortal eyes:
> And heaven's broad canopy of blue
> Hung bootless o'er the vanished view.
> Skilled natives of the neighbouring place,
> No vestiges, could ever trace:
> By landmarks, permanent, they told,
> Where would arise the enchanted hold.

Now where Hogg got this is a mystery. It is unlikely that, by 1827, he had encountered the obscure thirteenth-century fragment of the Oxford *Folie Tristran* (which may be the oldest reference). Hogg was well read and is more likely to have taken this from a printed source than to have picked it up as traditional, oral, folklore, but in fact his authority is unknown. No other Cornish writer has mentioned this. No Cornish folklorist, in this present century or in the previous one, collected for us any independently-attested legends about Tintagel.

King Arthur's Great Hall

Without question, today's premier Other Tintagel is the world manifest at King Arthur's Great Hall, a commercial establishment at the top or inland end of Tintagel village's one main street – called 'Fore Street', as main streets in Cornwall usually are. This story cries out for a book on its own, though it is far from certain that the necessary documentation survives. Frederick Thomas Glasscock, whose surname was pronounced 'Glasscock' or 'Glazzock', was a reputed near-millionaire. His money came from Monkhouse and Glasscock Ltd, makers of Monk and Glass brand custard-powders and jellies (older readers may recall their logo, a Friar Tuck figure clutching an hourglass). Mr Glasscock retired to Tintagel shortly after 1920, where he built a villa-style bungalow with magnificent views, a home that he named *Eirenikon* (Greek for 'peaceful (home), place of peace'). The local tale is that in the window of a

106 *Mr Glasscock's first (1929) King Arthur's Hall: the interior.*

village shop, Youlton's, he noticed alongside a pile of Monk and Glass products a replica of Excalibur or some such Arthurian object; explored the connection with Tintagel; and plunged headlong into the world of Arthur as a symbol of medieval chivalry and righteousness, a beacon in the decadent world of flapperdom, Black and Tans and bankrupt chicken-farmers. By the late 1920s he had bought a large old house, next to the Wharncliffe Arms hotel; a house said then to have 16 bedrooms but no bathroom. Immediately behind it, Glasscock built his first replica Hall of Chivalry, with a canopied throne, Round Table, box-like side chapels, Sword in the Stone, and a sequence of oil paintings commissioned from William Hatherell, RI (**106**). The Hall and its parent streetfront premises, opened to the public by 1929, was headquarters for an Order of the Fellowship of the Knights of the Round Table of King Arthur. Graded membership began with the under-14 Searchers – girls as well as boys; 'Maister Glazzock', it is sometimes said, was much taken with the lovely girls of the district. Searchers could progress to become Pilgrims, and ultimately to investiture as Knights. The ideals, firmly stated and recognizable as the Christian ethos in rather grandiose wording, were linked to the imagined world of Arthur as the pinnacle of medieval chivalry. In 1929, work began on a much larger Hall of Chivalry. This is not much smaller than the nave of many surviving medieval abbeys. Its complexity, high standard of construction and detailing, fittings and furnishings all show that its replacement value today would be a million (or

more) pounds. The long strip of land on which it sits may have been one of the burgage plots of thirteenth–fourteenth-century Tintagel. This interesting sidelight would have meant little to its founder, whose outlook became progressively more international.

The Hall, and its Fellowship, may have been at Tintagel because that was where the Glasscocks retired and because Tintagel proved to have a connection with Arthur; but that was all. F.T. Glasscock operated completely apart from all the not wholly dissimilar native Cornish movements that also arose in the 1920s – the network of Old Cornwall societies, the revivalist bardic college Gorseth Kernow (motto: *Nynsyu Marow Myghtern Arthur*, 'King Arthur Is Not Dead'), and the fund-raising 1929 Tintagel pageant. Glasscock's aims, the nature of his slightly secretive ceremonies and the intended audience, were misunderstood. Cornwall's Grand Bard, Henry Jenner (p. 54), loftily likened the Fellowship to 'such excellent institutions as the Boy Scouts, the Girl Guides, and the Rotary Clubs'. George Bishop of the Atlanta Boarding-House at Tintagel, secretary of the supporters' Round Table Club, rushed to the defence.

> To many here Mr Glasscock represents the spirit of King Arthur . . . Arthur still lives in Tintagel and faith in him will never waver here . . . Tintagel's poor and the local tradesfolk have every reason to bless the day that sent Mr Glasscock among us . . . The Fellowship has a hall larger and more magnificent than any local church . . . we shall get unity of worship and feel a real faith within us.

These were intentional digs at Jenner, known to be a High Church ritualist, for his public rebuttal of an Arthurian past at Tintagel (p. 55).

A quasi-religious outreach in the ideals and ambitions of Mr Glasscock's Fellowship is apparent from the literature. King Arthur's Hall published a steady output of brochures, postcards, pamphlets and even bound books, B.D. Vere's long verse play *King Arthur* among them. These, now hard to find, are the despair of bibliographers and of would-be historians because they were printed at Guildford, not always deposited with copyright libraries, seldom dated, and usually omitted any author's name (it is only an assumption that Glasscock himself wrote most of them (**107**)). The second

THE ORDER OF THE FELLOWSHIP OF THE KNIGHTS OF THE ROUND TABLE OF KING ARTHUR

KING ARTHUR'S HALL, TINTAGEL

KING ARTHUR'S HALL is a centre for all things in connection with, and has been founded to perpetuate the memory of, King Arthur and the Knights of the Round Table.

Arthur is a world-wide asset, and it is fitting that at Tintagel, the place where he was born, something should be in existence which will act as a centre to which the thoughts of people can turn and from which the necessary inspiration can be disseminated to enable the ideals associated with his name to be a living force for all time. To many Tintagel is a hallowed spot, and the increasing number of people who visit it each year solely because of its association with this wonderful early King testify to a desire to keep his ideals before them. The world would have been poorer in the past without King Arthur, and something less noble to-day and in the future.

Catalogue

of

Articles in Connection with King Arthur

To be Obtained at

KING ARTHUR'S HALL, TINTAGEL, ENGLAND

INDEX

(The copyright is strictly reserved in connection with the articles and groups marked with an asterisk.)

107 *A sample of Mr F.T. Glasscock's publications, around 1930, from King Arthur's Hall at Tintagel.*

Great Hall or Hall of Chivalry was opened in 1933. Any description would be a poor substitute for a personal inspection. Different types of stone from all over Cornwall, some from long disused quarries or rare veins, were used. The finest attribute is the group of nearly a hundred stained glass windows by Veronica Whall (1887–1967), daughter of Christopher Whall the Arts and Crafts master – Whall & Whall Ltd., Hammersmith. Masterpieces of secular art, her windows are the best modern depiction of the Arthur cycle and its figures, and must rank among Britain's finest stained glass of this century (**colour plate 9**).

Mr Glasscock died suddenly in 1934, on board the *Queen Mary*; he was sailing to found a North American branch. His widow outlived him for a few years, but Eirenikon is now a residential home for the elderly. In ill-documented circumstances the Fellowship came to a halt. The Great Hall and the premises were sold after the Second World War to a local Masonic lodge, who maintained the front part as a shop. An enviable library of Arthuriana, Celtic works and medieval literature had been built up – no expense spared – as part of the infrastructure. Some of it remains, but the plums were sold long since. Happily, today King Arthur's Great Hall of Chivalry has a new and caring tenant; it is well-presented and cherished, and there is talk of reviving the Fellowship in a contemporary guise.

It is easy to poke fun at the whole place as a custard millionaire's folly. Resist that temptation. It would be shallow and unjust to do so. A visit to the Great Hall evokes admiration, even awe. Frederick Glasscock, remembered as a small, dynamic and sometimes peppery man, was a genuine philanthropist. He arrived in Tintagel when the parish, like most of Cornwall, had reached economic rock-bottom – Cornish unemployment figures arouse no interest in Whitehall, then or today. Glasscock provided new trade, employment for the stone-masons, hope and excitement. He founded youth clubs and sporting facilities, and built a village hall at nearby Treknow. The only known fly in the ointment was an unhappy and complicated court case between Glasscock and Miss Whall concerning payment for her stained-glass windows. It is impossible to fault his clearly-expressed moral ideals. One could guess that they manifested that post-First World War yearning for peace and a new moral order which gave rise to the League of Nations. The very house-name Eirenikon points that way; had he fought in the trenches, lost a son in Flanders, experienced personal tragedy?

This particular Other Tintagel will never be repeated. Its outward expression is as much a part of Tintagel's archaeology as the Castle, or the parish church, and just as worthy of study. Indignant at Jenner's casual suggestion that King Arthur had no historical link with Cornwall, or at any rate none with Tintagel, Glasscock wanted to ensure that 'the knowledge of this glorious heritage of Cornwall be transmitted to future generations', and his opinion was that Henry Jenner was trying 'to throw away one of the greatest beauties that Cornwall possesses'. We can be wholly confident that Mr Glasscock, had he succeeded Kinsman in the archaic office of Constable, would never have permitted – as today's less sensitive administrators unhappily did – the use of the Castle, for payment, as the venue of a television conjurer's tasteless performance. A drawback was the Fellowship's chosen isolation, cultural as much as geographical, with its dependence upon the personality of the founder. Only those fully familiar with Cornwall and the Cornish as they were in the 1930s will realize that one of Glasscock's obstacles to acceptance outside Tintagel lay in the fact that he was not himself a Cornishman. This does not excuse some shabby treatment. When in 1933 Jenner was invited to the formal opening of the Great Hall, he found some reason to decline, and then wrote that 'had I been able to be present, I should certainly not have worn bardic robes or taken any part officially as Grand Bard'.

Tintagel today

The shape of Tintagel village in the 1990s, most rewardingly studied during July and August when the day's intake of cars and coaches has arrived, proffers an object lesson in rural economy and in the effectiveness (or otherwise) of all post-1947 planning legislation. This may be an Other Tintagel, intimately linked to the presence of the supposedly Arthurian past, that we could wish to overlook. A privately-commissioned survey (August 1988), posing separate questionnaires to a 10 per cent sample of residents, and also to 185 visitors, unearthed a lot of interesting news. Though neither visitors nor residents care very much for the present look of the village – many of the latter believe it is the price to be paid for dependence on a part-year tourist economy – nearly a third of visitors had come to Tintagel for the shops (!) and had no intention of walking down the valley to visit the Castle or Island. However, though significant numbers of all respondents admitted that they did not really believe in a historical Arthur, or (if they did) that he had a genuine connection with the place, this left quite unaffected their plans to see the ancient monuments, or to have included Tintagel in a wider holiday itinerary.

One set of responses during this 1988 survey must lead us from Tintagel Past – back-cloth to all the Other Tintagels just explored – to

108 *Midsummer 1992: a popular innovation at Tintagel Castle. A professional story-teller was engaged to take tours, during which he recounted Arthurian tales in dramatic fashion.*

Tintagel Future, which to the archaeologist, historian, conservationist and social economist will primarily mean the management and development of Tintagel's visible attractions. But here the present writer, in several of these capacities and also as a Cornishman, must in fairness dissociate himself from the organizations, public and private, to which he belongs, and make it plain that he writes purely as an individual. The 1988 responses to questions were united in criticizing the presentation of Tintagel Castle (and Island) as an ancient monument where an entry fee is charged. The absence of such guidance is not the fault of the archaeologists, whose record of prompt publication of all post-1980 results stands comparison with the best. In the various surveys commissioned by English Heritage, surveys that commonly end with managerial recommendations, the need for publicly-visible interpretation has invariably been stressed. We may all express the hope that reaction to so obvious a need will soon take concrete form (**108**).

Looking at visitor-totals, Tintagel had by 1989 climbed to sixth position in the long list of all such Properties In Care in England. Visitors would probably understand more about environmental conservation if they were given explanatory notices, but Tintagel is one of a group of sites (possibly a minority in its own region) where understanding of any aspect

109 *The lower terrace on Site C: University of Glasgow team at work, Spring 1991.*

110 *The lower terrace on Site C, Spring 1991; for the first time what appears to be a genuine post-Roman walling is exposed by excavation.*

remains limited, simply because we do not know enough about what happened there. And that, inevitably, points to the need for further exploration (**109**); perhaps within a future plan where funds for excavation equal or even exceed those for maintenance and non-archaeological enhancement (**110**).

The Future Tintagel that should be our common goal is therefore a monument presented, excitingly and in intelligible ways (and from 1992 in several languages). That should not prohibit any mention of the Arthurian connection, provided it is made clear that the Arthur of the twelfth century is a literary and not an archaeological concept. It should also be a monument where, because it is acceptable to make an increased income through charging more for an enhanced product, the task of finding out more about what the monument *is* continues to have a claim on funds. Finally, the whole presentation of Tintagel should stress the geographically-immediate past of Cornwall, as well as that of administrative England. This is rather more than a case of localized sentiment. In a hypothetical scale of 'ownership' Tintagel belongs first and foremost to the Duchy of Cornwall; then to the Cornish people; then to unified Great Britain with its amalgam of the English and the older Celtic-speaking peoples; and finally to Europe because Tintagel Past is also quite an important demonstration of parts of Europe's past.

Last of all, is it possible to find a patch of common territory between the two concepts of Tintagel – Other, and Future? Must all the mysteries be flung out in the cause of Culture,

Academic Integrity and Europe 1992? The answers are Yes to the first, No to the second. This book, a progress report confined to what field-workers think are facts and supportable inferences, has to build historical models solely out of those facts or inferences. The models try to answer questions that start with How? When? and Where? Very occasionally they can deal with Who? but questions beginning Why? can only be met by guessing. Here are some things that nobody at the moment can answer. Why are there no signs of prehistoric activity or occupation on the Island? Why is the Footprint *there*, and not on some inland carn or a rock within a hillfort? What were people doing on the Island in the Roman period? Why was the Tunnel really hacked out ('medieval larder' is actually no more than a best guess)? What on earth is that 23-m (75-ft) long building next to Site D and what is its date? Why does the almost-inaccessible cavern alongside the Iron Gate rocks have cut steps leading to it and remains of a cross-wall, and what went on in there – and when? These are for starters. There are other little problems that might seem to be technical and archaeological but are in fact very much human-interest ones. All the references to the hundred or more imported Mediterranean amphorae had to skate around the question of what they contained, because so far we do not know. But there are research techniques, now being applied, able to detect the former presence of fatty liquids like olive oil or certain substances used to doctor wine; and it may be that these will provide answers. The jars can hardly have come so far simply as empty containers. And now the discovery that the imports include, besides jars and dishes, pottery that looks far more like the galley-furnishings of a sixth-century Mediterranean ship raises other questions. Why has similar pottery never been found at other relevant British or Irish sites? Why trade it, anyway? Was this a private venture by a ship's cook; or was one of these ships wrecked in the Haven and, if so, can sub-aqua exploration off the Iron Gate rocks – tried out in 1990–1 and found to be practicable – hope to find such traces?

Architects who build avant-garde dwellings do so for the pleasure of designing and creating them, not for having to live in them (or not for long). Honest archaeologists will probably admit that they live and work for the exploration, the exercise of skills and the deployment of experience, not for the frozen result. That whole process of exploration is what most interests the ordinary, sane, non-archaeological visitor. At Tintagel – Island, Castle, church-yard and district – there is every indication that exploration has so far gone only a short distance.

Further reading

The bibliography by chapters will cover virtually all the topics mentioned. Cornwall, measuring roughly 20 by 73 km (12 by 80 miles), is too small a region for piece-meal treatment; there is no such thing as an Early History of *North* Cornwall, very roughly the stretch from Padstow to Bude (with Tintagel in the middle). The best general work on the background to Periods III and IV is Canon L.E. Elliott-Binns, *Medieval Cornwall* (Methuen, 1955), and a concise archaeology and history update for this is the chapter 'Medieval Cornwall' by Ann Preston-Jones and Peter Rose, pp. 135–85 (with illus.) in *Cornish Archaeology* 25 (1986), ISSN 0070 024X. The entire Early Christian side of Period II, with the supporting evidence for which there is no room here, is covered in C. Thomas, *And Shall These Mute Stones Speak?* (University of Wales Press, Cardiff 1993), linking south and south-west Wales with south-west Britain. As for Tintagel itself, even today a comprehensive study of all the discoveries, and all the background historical details and documents used by Sir John Maclean in the nineteenth century and Canon A.C. Canner in the twentieth, would make a very large book; presumably there will eventually be one, but not while there is any prospect of excavations at the Island or churchyard continuing.

A high proportion of visitors always state their interest in the natural history of the district. A good broad picture of Cornwall is Rennie Bere's *The Nature of Cornwall* (Barracuda, Buckingham 1982: 0 86023 163 1). The botany, exceptionally fully studied and relevant to all periods at Tintagel, is set out in L.J. Margetts and R.W. David, *A Review of the Cornish Flora 1980* (Institute of Cornish Studies, Redruth 1981: 0 903686 34 1), recently brought up to date in L.J. Margetts and K.L. Spurgin, *The Cornish Flora Supplement 1981–1990* (Trendrine Press, Zennor, St Ives, 1991: 0 9512562 2 X).

1 Space, time and discourses

The Duchy: Crispin Gill (ed.), *The Duchy of Cornwall* (David & Charles, Newton Abbot 1987), chaps. 1 and 2.

The parish: Arthur C. Canner, *The Parish of Tintagel. Some Historical Notes* (1982, reprinted Tintagel 1992).

William Taylor, *History of Tintagel, Compiled from Ancient Records and Modern Writers* (Blackford, Truro 1927).

Milestones: R.G. Collingwood and R.P. Wright, *The Roman Inscriptions of Britain, I. Inscriptions on Stone* (Oxford, 1965), nos. 2230, 2231.

The first Christians: Charles Thomas, *And Shall These Mute Stones Speak?* (University of Wales Press, Cardiff 1993).

Earl Richard: N. Denholm-Young, *Richard of Cornwall* (Blackwell, Oxford, 1947).

O.J. Padel, 'Tintagel in the Twelfth and Thirteenth Centuries', *Cornish Studies* 16 (1989), 61–6.

The churches: Edward H. Sedding, *Norman Architecture in Cornwall* (Ward & Co., London 1909), Tintagel, 382–90, Minster, 286–7.

Bottreaux family: Sir John Maclean, *Parochial & Family History of the Deanery of Trigg Minor . . . Cornwall* (Nichols & Son, London, 3 vols. 1868–79), i. 631–41.

Royal earls: E.B. Fryde *et al.* (eds.), *Handbook of British Chronology*, 3rd ed. (Royal Historical Society, London 1986).

2 Magical conception, modern misconceptions
Geoffrey of Monmouth: O.J. Padel, 'Geoffrey of Monmouth and Cornwall', *Cambridge Medieval Celtic Studies* 8 (1984), 1–28.
Geoffrey of Monmouth, History of the Kings of Britain, transl. S. Evans, rev. C.W. Dunn (Everyman Library, 1963).
William Worcestre: John H. Harvey (ed.), *William Worcestre. Itineraries* (Oxford, 1969).
John Leland: Lucy Toulmin Smith (ed.), *Leland's Itinerary in England and Wales*, new ed., 5 vols. (Centaur Press, 1964), vol. i.
John Norden: *Speculi Britanniae Pars, A Topographical and Historical Description of Cornwall* (Bateman, London 1728).
William Ravenhill (ed. and intro.), *John Norden's Manuscript Maps of Cornwall and Its Nine Hundreds* (University of Exeter, 1972).
Richard Carew: *The Survey of Cornwall* (John Jaggard, London 1602). F.E. Halliday (ed. & intro.), *Richard Carew of Antony, The Survey of Cornwall, etc.* (Andrew Melrose, London 1953).
Parliamentary survey: Norman J.G. Pounds (ed.), *The Parliamentary Survey of the Duchy of Cornwall, Part II* (Devon & Cornwall Record Soc., n.s. vol. 27, Torquay 1984).
Francis Kilvert: Richard Maber & Angela Tregonning (eds.), *Kilvert's Cornish Diary, Journal no. 4 1870* (Alison Hodge, Penzance 1989).
Mining: A K. Hamilton Jenkin, *Mines and Miners of Cornwall: XIV, St Austell to Saltash* (Truro Bookshop, Truro 1967).
Slate quarrying: Adam Sharpe, *Coastal Slate Quarries, Tintagel to Trebarwith* (Cornwall Archaeological Unit, Truro 1990).
First excavation: J.J. Wilkinson, 'Tintagel Castle', *Journal of the Royal Institution of Cornwall*, 3 (Truro 1871), 225–35.
Guidebooks: T.C. Paris (in part), *A Handbook for Travellers in Devon and Cornwall*, 1st ed. (John Murray, London 1850).
W.J.C. Armstrong, *A Rambler's Guide to Tintagel and Camelford* 1st ed. – (Blackford, Truro 1931); 2nd ed. (Plymouth 1935).
Beatrix F. Creswell, *The North Cornwall Coast, Homeland Handbooks 72* 1st ed. (Homeland Association & Fredk. Warne, London 1908).
The railway dimension: Roger Burdett Wilson, *Go Great Western. A History of GWR Publicity* (David & Charles, Newton Abbot 1970).

3 'Stepped at one stride across the sea . . .'
General: C. Thomas, 'Minor Sites at Tintagel Island', *Cornish Studies* 16 (1989), 31–43.
Geology (unrevised): E.C. Freshney *et al.*, *Geology of the Coast between Tintagel and Bude* (HMSO, 1972). M.C. McKeown *et al.*, *Geology of the Country around Boscastle and Holsworthy* (HMSO, 1972).
Domesday survey of 1086: C. and F. Thorn (eds.), *Domesday Book: 10, Cornwall* (Phillimore, Chichester 1979).
Place-names: O.J. Padel, *Cornish Place-Name Elements* (English Place-Name Society, vol. LVI/LVII) (EPNS, Nottingham 1985).
Shipping: C.L. Todd Gray, *Early-Stuart Mariners and Shipping. The Maritime Surveys of Devon and Cornwall 1619–35* (Devon & Cornwall Record Society, n.s. vol. 33) (DCRS, Exeter 1990).
Sea-levels: C. Thomas, *Exploration of a Drowned Landscape. Archaeology and History of the Isles of Scilly* (Batsford, London 1985), chaps. 1 and 2.
Folk-lore: Robert Hunt FRS, *Popular Romances of the West of England*, 2nd ed. (J.C. Hotten, London 1871).
'King Arthur's Cups & Saucers': plan and note, A. Preston-Jones, in *Cornish Archaeology* 26 (1987), 83.
Maclean's plans of Tintagel: Sir John Maclean, *Trigg Minor* (see Chapter 1), iii. 185–276, plates.
Grenville's plan, notes and 'rampiers': C.S. Gilbert, *An Historical Survey of the County of Cornwall*, 3 vols. (Congdon, Plymouth Dock 1817–20), iii. 580 ff. J.J. Wilkinson, 'Tintagel Castle', *Journal of the Royal Institution of Cornwall* 3 (1871), 225–35 (reproduces plan); H.M. Whitley, 'Note to accompany Sir Richard Grenville's Plott of Tintagel Castle', *ibid.*, 8 (1885), 269.

4 'The Office of Works had decided to uncover . . .'
Original guidebook: C.A. Ralegh Radford, *Tintagel Castle, Cornwall*, 1st ed. – (HMSO, 1935, repr. 1936–37; 2nd ed., 1939; reprints to 18th impression 1979), re-issued by English Heritage, 1985.
Local archaeology: C. Thomas, 'The Fiftieth Anniversary of the West Cornwall Field Club', *Cornish Archaeology* 24 (1985), 5–14.
Jenner's lecture: Henry Jenner, 'Tintagel Castle in History and Romance', *Journal of the*

Royal Institution of Cornwall, 22 (1927), 190–200.

Reports: C.A.R. Radford, 'Tintagel; the castle and Celtic monastery – interim report', *Antiquaries Journal* 15 (1935), 401–19. Radford, 'Tintagel in History and Legend', *Journal of the Royal Institution of Cornwall* 25 (1942), appendix, 26–41. Radford, 'The Celtic Monastery in Britain', *Archaeologia Cambrensis* 111 (1962), 1–24. (See also K.R. Dark, 'The Plan and Interpretation of Tintagel', *Cambridge Medieval Celtic Studies* 9 (1985), 1–17.)

Imported pottery: C.A. Ralegh Radford, 'Imported Pottery found at Tintagel, Cornwall', in: D.B. Harden (ed.), *Dark-Age Britain* (Methuen, London 1956), 59–70. C. Thomas, 'Some Imported Post-Roman Sherds in Cornwall and their Origin', *Proc. West Cornwall Field Club* 2.i (1957), 15–22. C. Thomas, 'Imported Pottery in Dark-Age Western Britain', *Medieval Archaeology* 3 (1959), 89–111. J.W. Hayes, *Late Roman Pottery* (British School at Rome, London 1972), and *Supplement* (ditto, 1980). D.P.S. Peacock and D.F. Williams, *Amphorae and the Roman Economy* (Longman, London and NY 1986). C. Thomas, *A Provisional List of Imported Pottery in Post-Roman Western Britain and Ireland (Special Report 7)* (Institute of Cornish Studies, Redruth 1981).

Tintagel churchyard 1942: C. Thomas, 'The archaeology of Tintagel parish churchyard', *Cornish Studies* 16 (1989), 79–92.

5 Deconstruction of a monastery

Cataloguing of finds, 1988: see introduction to *Further Reading*.

Mothecombe, Devon, sherd with (?)XXV graffito: *Transactions of the Devonshire Association* 93 (1961), 79–80.

Reassessment: C. Thomas, 'East, and West: Tintagel Mediterranean Imports and the Early Insular Church', in: S.M. Pearce (ed.), *The Early Church in Western Britain and Ireland* (BAR Brit. ser. 102, Oxford 1982), 17–34. Ian Burrow, 'Tintagel – Some Problems', *Scottish Archaeological Forum* 5, for 1973 (Edinburgh 1974), 99–103 (with Radford's comments, 136–9). See also C.A.R. Radford and M.J. Swanton, *Arthurian Sites in the West* (University of Exeter, Exeter 1975), chap. ii, 'Tintagel'.

The 'Burnt Area', 1985 survey, and implications: C. Thomas and P.J. Fowler, 'Tintagel: A New Survey of the Island', *Annual Review 1984–85* (Royal Commission on the Historical Monuments of England, London 1985). 16–22, with map. C. Thomas, *Tintagel Castle* (guide) (English Heritage, 1986 and reprints). C. Thomas, 'Tintagel Castle', *Antiquity* 62 (1988), 421–34.

6 Models for the moment: Roman and post-Roman Tintagel

Roman south-west: Malcolm Todd, *The South-West to AD 1000* (Longman, London & NY 1987).

Roman milestones: R.G. Collingwood and R.P. Wright, *The Roman Inscriptions of Britain. I. Inscriptions on Stone* (Clarendon Press, Oxford 1965).

Place-names: A.L.F. Rivet and Colin Smith, *The Placenames of Roman Britain* (Batsford, London 1979).

Tin production: R.D. Penhallurick, *Tin in Antiquity* (Institute of Metals, London 1986).

Early routes: R.G. Collingwood, 'Roman Milestones in Cornwall', *Antiquaries Journal* 4 (1924), 101–12. I.D. Margary, *Roman Roads in Britain*, 3rd ed. (John Baker, London 1973), chap. 3.

Early shipping: L. Casson, *Ships and seamanship in the Ancient World* (Princeton University Press, Princeton NJ 1971). A.H.M. Jones, *The Later Roman Empire 284–602* (Blackwell, Oxford 1964).

Trade: C. Thomas, 'The Context of Tintagel. A New Model for the Diffusion of Post-Roman Mediterranean Imports', *Cornish Archaeology* 27 (1988), 7–25. M.G. Fulford, 'Byzantium and Britain: a Mediterranean perspective on Post-Roman Mediterranean Imports in Western Britain and Ireland', *Medieval Archaeology* 33 (1989), 106. P. Arthur, 'Amphorae and the Byzantine World', in J-Y. Empereur and Y. Garlan (eds.), *Recherches sur les amphores grecques* (= Supplement XIII, Bulletin de correspondence Hellenique) (Athens 1986), pp. 655–60.

Citadels, centres of power, etc.: M.R. Nieke and H.B. Duncan, 'Dalriada; the establishment and maintenance of an Early Historic kingdom in Northern Britain', in S.T. Driscoll and M.R. Nieke (eds.), *Power and Politics in Early Medieval Britain and Ireland* (Edinburgh University Press, Edinburgh 1988), pp. 6–21. L.A. Alcock, 'The activities of potentates in Celtic Britain, AD 500–800: a positivist approach', *ibid.*, pp. 22–46. L.A. Alcock, *Bede, Eddius and the Forts of the North Britons* (Jarrow Lecture

1988) (Jarrow 1989). L.A. and E.A. Alcock, 'Reconnaissance excavations on Early Historic fortifications and other royal sites in Scotland, 1874–84: 4, Excavations at Alt Clut, Clyde Rock, Strathclyde, 1974–75', *Proceedings of the Society of Antiquaries of Scotland*, 120 (1990), 95–150. Thomas Charles-Edwards, 'Early medieval kingships in the British Isles', in S. Bassett (ed.), *The Origins of Anglo-Saxon Kingdoms* (Leicester University Press, Leicester 1989), 28–39.

The Footprint: J.R.C. Hamilton, *Excavations at Clickhimin, Shetland* (HMSO, Edinburgh, 1968), 150–6, discussion with references.

7 Models for the moment: the churchyard, pre-Conquest and medieval times

Tintagel parish churchyard: C. Thomas, 'The Archaeology of Tintagel Parish Churchyard', *Cornish Studies* 16 (1988), 79–92. J.A. Nowakowski and C. Thomas, *The Churchyard Excavations at Tintagel Parish Church, North Cornwall, Spring 1990* (CAU, Truro 1990); Idem, *Grave News From Tintagel. An illustrated account of Archaeological Excavations at Tintagel Churchyard, Cornwall*, 1991 (CAU, Truro 1992).

Christian beginnings: C. Thomas, *Christianity in Roman Britain to AD 500* (Batsford, London 1981; 2nd rev. impr., 1985). C. Thomas, *And Shall These Mute Stones Speak?* (University of Wales Press, Cardiff 1993).

Early cemetery enclosures: C. Thomas, *The Early Christian Archaeology of North Britain* (Oxford University Press, London Glasgow & NY 1971), chaps 3 and 4. Ann Preston-Jones, 'Decoding Cornish Churchyards', in Nancy Edwards and Alan Lane (eds.), *The Early Church in Wales and the West* (Oxbow Books, Oxford 1992), 102–24.

Primary Christian art: C. Thomas, *The Early Christian Archaeology of North Britain*, chap. 4. C. Thomas, 'The Earliest Christian art in Ireland and Britain', in Michael Ryan (ed.), *Ireland and Insular Art AD 500–1200* (Royal Irish Academy, Dublin 1987), 7–11.

Minsters: John Blair (ed.), *Minsters and Parish Churches. The Local Church in Transition 950–1200* (Monograph no. 17) (Oxford University Committee for Archaeology, Oxford 1988). John Blair and Richard Sharpe (eds.), *Pastoral Care Before the Parish* (Leicester University Press, Leicester 1992).

Monasteries: B. Lynette Olson, *Early Monasteries in Cornwall* (Boydell Press, Woodbridge 1989).

Potterne font: Norman Davey, 'A Pre-Conquest Church and Baptistery at Potterne', *Wilts. Archaeological Magazine* 59 (1964), 116–23.

Juliot and other saints: S. Baring-Gould and John Fisher, *The Lives of the British Saints*, 4 vols. (Hon. Soc. of Cymmrodorion, London 1913).

The 1988 CAU surveys: *Tintagel Castle. Survey and Excavation at the Inner Ward, the Chapel, Site 4 and the Garden* (Nic Appleton, Tricia Fox, Andy Waters), 2 pts. Unpublished; Cornwall Archaeological Unit, Truro 1988.

Late pre-Conquest inscribed stones; Arthur G. Langdon, 'Early Christian Monuments', in William Page (ed.), *The Victoria History of the County of Cornwall, Volume One* (James Street, London 1906), 407–50 illus.

Medieval pottery: C. O'Mahoney, *The Medieval Pottery from Tintagel* (Special Report no.8) (Institute of Cornish Studies, Redruth 1989).

Incised slates: Carl M. Thorpe, 'Incised Pictorial Slates from Tintagel', *Cornish Studies* 16 (1988), 69–78; further examples shown in the 1990 and 1991 reports, Nowakowski & Thomas 1991, 1992 (see above).

Bossiney mound, etc.; Canner, *The Parish of Tintagel* (1992), chaps. 2, 6–11. Michael Williams, *Tintagel*, 2nd edn. (Bossiney Books, St Teath 1980), 16 ff. Ann Preston-Jones & Peter Rose, 'Medieval Cornwall', *Cornish Archaeology* 25 (1986), 135–85.

Castle records: Maclean, *Trigg Minor*, iii. 185 ff. (see notes to Chap. 1).

Period II below Great Hall: C. Thomas, 'CAU Excavations at Tintagel Island, 1988: The Discoveries and their Implications', *Cornish Studies* 16 (1988), 49–60.

8 Other, and future, Tintagels

Arthurian beliefs and sites in Cornwall: W.H. Dickinson, *King Arthur in Cornwall* (Longmans Green and Co., London 1900). Brenda Duxbury and Michael Williams, *King Arthur Country in Cornwall* (Bossiney Books, St. Teath 1979). Incident of 1113: R.V. Elliott-Binns, *Medieval Cornwall* (Methuen, London 1955), pp. 261–2.

Tristan cycle: Texts – Alfred Ewert, (ed.), *The Romance of Tristran*, vol. I, text (Blackwell, Oxford 1939). Guy R. Mermier, *Beroul. Tristran and Yseut.* (American University

Studies, ser. II, 50) (Peter Lang, NY and Paris 1987). Alan S. Fedrick, *The Romance of Tristan by Beroul* (Penguin Classics, 1970). A.T. Hatto, *Gottfried von Strassburg. Tristan, with the 'Tristan' of Thomas* (Penguin Classics, 1960). Commentary – O.J. Padel, 'The Cornish Background of the Tristan Stories', *Cambridge Medieval Celtic Studies* 1 (1981), 53–81. W.J. McCann, 'Tristan: The Celtic material re-examined', in A. Stevens and R. Wisbey (eds.), *Gottfried von Strassburg and the Medieval Tristan Legend* (Brewer/Inst. of Germanic Stud., Cambridge/London 1990), 19–28.

Arthurian revival: Roger Simpson, *Camelot Regained. The Arthurian Revival and Tennyson 1800–1849* (Arthurian Studies XXI) (Brewer, Cambridge 1990).

Other works cited: Thomas Hogg, *The Fabulous History of the Ancient Kingdom of Cornwall* (Longman Rees Orme and Co., London 1827). Richard Seddon, *The Mystery of Arthur at Tintagel* (Rudolf Steiner Press, London 1990). Paul Broadhurst, *Tintagel and the Arthurian, Mythos* (Pendragon Press, Launceston 1992).

King Arthur's Great Hall 1929: (F.T. Glass-cock?) *The Book of the Order of the Fellowship of the Knights of the Round Table of King Arthur* (K.A.'s Hall, Tintagel n.d. = 1930?). *Catalogue of Articles in Connection with King Arthur*, 16 pp. (K.A.'s Hall, Tintagel, n.d. = 1932?). B.D. Vere, *King Arthur. His Symbolic Story in Verse* (K.A.'s Hall, Tintagel 1930).

Veronica Whall's glass: Veronica Whall, *Stained Glass Windows in King Arthur's Hall Tintagel*, brochure (Whall and Wall Ltd., Hammersmith, London W.6, 1932). Peter Cormack, *Women Stained Glass Artists of the Arts and Crafts Movement* – exhibition catalogue 1985–6 (William Morris Gallery, Walthamstow, London E.17, 1985), 17–19. Muriel Whitaker, *The Legends of King Arthur in Art* (Brewer, Cambridge 1990), 314–16.

Visiting Tintagel

Cornwall's principal museum is the former county museum and art gallery, since 1991 the Royal Cornwall Museum, which is combined with the Royal Institution of Cornwall's premises, offices, stores and Courtney Library at River Street, Truro (telephone (0872) 72205). The museum is open Monday–Saturday, 9 to 5, and charges a small admission fee to non-members.

All moveable objects found on or below the ground within Tintagel Castle and Island are the property of the Duchy of Cornwall, and under an arrangement dating from the 1940s these are deposited at the Royal Institution of Cornwall. No place in Cornwall could really be described as 'central' because of Cornwall's shape, but the City of Truro with its cathedral and county hall is the recognized capital served by road and rail (and boat, if you travel from Falmouth). It has long been firm policy to discourage the formation of archaeological collections in Cornish museums other than the Royal Cornwall Museum, while accepting that there are a few old-established collections elsewhere (Penlee House, Penzance; Isles of Scilly Museum). All the Tintagel material is therefore at Truro. At the time of writing (1992), and as part of ongoing expansion and reorganization of the RCM, new Tintagel displays are being planned; but there is now far too much material for it all to be put on show. Stored finds are accessible for study to serious researchers though advance notice of any visit to see them is essential. While it might seem a good idea to have an archaeological museum at Tintagel itself, it really forms no part of the remit of either the Duchy or English Heritage. Problems of premises, finance, staffing, conservation and registration would be too formidable.

Archaeological work within Tintagel Churchyard takes place, as in 1990 and 1991, within the terms of a Faculty issued by the Chancellor of the Diocese (and of course the prior agreement of the incumbent and the parochial church council). Small finds here, the quantity of which is much less than from the Island or Castle, belong to the Church. Until a final report is prepared, the various churchyard finds are held on loan at Truro by Cornwall Archaeological Unit.

Not all of the Tintagel excavation papers, work-notes, records accompanying commissioned surveys, and catalogues of finds (including the very large 1988 *Catalogue No.1*, of all finds other than medieval pottery) are published, nor is it intended to do so. Archive copies of most of them are held in London by the National Archaeological Record, which is maintained by the Royal Commission on the Historical Monuments of England, Fortress House, 23 Savile Row, London W1X 2JQ. These are open to public consultation. The Commission's National Monuments Record library at Fortress House, similarly open and with its main collection classified by English counties and parishes, has a large collection of photographs of Tintagel. Tintagel archive material, covering far more than could conceivably be published, is available for consultation (with prior notice) at Cornwall Archaeological Unit, Old County Hall, Station Road, Truro, Cornwall.

As for the sites mentioned in the text, the best things in life are still free and they include the freedom to walk along the National Coastal footpath around virtually the entire coastline of Cornwall, with free access to Tintagel parish church (which is open daily) and the other churches mentioned (some of which are kept locked against thieves, but with keyholders indicated). Tintagel Castle with the Island as a Property in Care, Mr Glasscock's Hall(s) of Chivalry as a concern that must pay its way and the Royal Cornwall Museum as a matter of policy, all charge something for entrance; fees are all less than half what it costs to enter Cornwall's numerous theme parks and similar attractions, some of which (August 1992) are teetering on the brink of insolvency. There are at least two good bookshops in Tintagel village, concentrating on Celtic, Arthurian and New Age subjects. North Cornwall District Council's Heritage Coast Service (from 1985) publishes a wonderful range of cheap guides and leaflets; one set gives detailed walks all over the district, and another describes just about every aspect of it, past and present, alive or dead. There are during the summer both Heritage Coast centres and travelling information-caravans; details can be obtained from their office in Bodmin, telephone (0208) 74121 extension 239. The National Trust administers in Fore Street, Tintagel, the Old Post Office – a fine example of a fifteenth-century substantial home, of a burgess rather than a farmer (free to members, otherwise small charge) – and sells its own excellent series of Cornwall coastal guides. Those for the Tintagel area are essential reading. The serious visitor, who wants to get a better grasp of this part of Cornwall during our Periods III and IV, should certainly include the churches of Lanteglos, Trevalga, Forrabury and Minster in any brief tour, and preferably the Duchy castles (adminstered by English Heritage) at Launceston, and at Restormel just outside Lostwithiel.

Glossary

amphora Large pottery containers, usually for liquids, with two handles and a narrow neck.

aquifer Natural source of groundwater, usually rainwater.

archaeomagnetic dating Technique for establishing approximate dates, BC or AD, by calculating variations in magnetic fields.

battens Smaller timbers used in constructing roofs, etc.

chamfered Worked or smoothed to a surface at an angle to adjacent surfaces.

coigns Dressed stones forming a built corner to a wall or construction.

corbelled A false dome; rows of overlapping stones or slabs set in rings, eventually closing or roofing a hemisphere.

demesne Land held or occupied by the possessors of any central establishment, instead of being leased to tenants.

flange-rim bowls Bowls or dishes with flattened protruding rims all round to facilitate lifting when full.

freestone Exposed bedrock of any kind, used for rough building.

galena A low-grade lead ore, in Cornwall usually mined from exposures on sea cliffs.

manciple In a medieval household, the official who arranges to buy or obtain all the food for meals.

micaceous ware Pottery whose clay contains particles of mica, giving it a slightly sparkling look.

mortarium In Roman times, a large pottery bowl studded with grits used in preparing vegetables for meals.

radiocarbon The radioactive (C14) counterpart of ordinary (C12) carbon, measurements of the decay of which can give calculated approximate dates BC and AD.

rampier Obsolete military term for a small blockhouse, bulwark, or defensive post.

slipware Commercially-produced pottery coated before firing with a slip or wash to produce a required final colour.

souterrain In parts of Atlantic Britain, Ireland and France, walled or rock-cut underground passages and chambers (mostly prehistoric) of uncertain purpose, but including use as store-houses.

tin-streaming As an older and simpler alternative to shaft, or hardrock, mining, the recovery of tin ore particles from the lowest gravels in stream-beds which are then smelted into ingots.

tympanum Filled semicircular stone surface, usually sculptured, above a built Norman doorway.

Index

INDEX